# SMALL TO GREAT

## HOW TO TURN YOUR SMALL BUSINESS INTO A GREAT BUSINESS

FREE DOWNLOADS TO GET YOUR BUSINESS MOVING!

Learn how two ordinary Australians achieved extraordinary success and transformed their small suburban business into a thriving national group, which today remains one of the fastest-growing businesses in their field.

ED CHAN and DAVID NAYLOR

www.chan-naylor.com.au

THE CHAN AND NAYLOR STORY

*Small to Great ... How to turn your small business into a great business*

Published by
CNIP Pty Ltd
Suite 5, Level 2, 55 Grandview Street Pymble
NSW 2073, Australia
Phone 02 9391 5000
www.chan-naylor.com.au
First Printed 2005
This edition published in 2018



National Library of Australia Cataloguing-in-Publication entry

| | |
|---|---|
| Authors: | Chan, Edward Sai-Ping, 1959- |
| | Naylor, David |
| Title: | How to Achieve Wealth for Life through Property Investing / Edward Chan. |
| ISBN: | 978-0-6482583-1-5 (pbk.) |
| Subjects: | Small business--Australia--Management. |
| | Small business--Growth. |
| Dewey Number: | 658.020994 |

Cover Design by Synchromesh Marketing & Creative Communications
Typeset by Working Type Studio — www.workingtype.com.au

## DAVID'S ACKNOWLEDGEMENT

**I dedicate this book to the following:**

My dad and mum, John and Margaret, who brought me into this world, cared for me, supported me through good and bad, loved me unconditionally. They gave me the inspiration to make my way in this world... words could never express my gratitude.

To my beautiful wife Dianne, who is my sounding board, and my sons Ben and Jordy, you have sacrificed much whilst I have built a business. I love you all dearly and you have given me purpose each day to meet the challenges head on. You are my pillars of strength and hopefully I can repay you for time lost in the coming years.

To the clients who have challenged my professionalism and have been loyal, and who without Chan & Naylor would not be where it is today... thank you.

Also, my sincerest thanks go to our alliance partners who have been supportive and assisted in our success to date. in particular Michael Yardney and his professional team from Metropole Property group. Brad Maunsell and Des Whyte (EKnowhow Accounting).

Alan Osrin, Michael Smith and Gary Weisz from Sage/Handisoft A huge thank you to the loyal hardworking and professional team at Chan & Naylor. From the administration staff right through to our partners, we would not have been able to achieve what we have — nor will be able to achieve our lofty goals for the future — without you.

And last of all to Ed... for his patience, determination, hard work and mentorship over the last 25-plus years of my life. It just goes to show you that good old fashion hard work pays off. We are the living example of the power of leverage: 1 + 1 really does equal three.

## ED'S ACKNOWLEDGEMENT

A success story of this significance could not have been achieved without the help of many people. First and foremost, to my wife and three children who have put up with the hours and weeks and months of my absence from home, whilst I travelled around Australia presenting seminars and attending meetings and working very long hours — thank you.

I'd like to acknowledge the many thousands of clients who have believed in us and stuck by us through the good times and bad times.

To our dedicated staff — without your hard work, we would not have such happy and loyal clients — and to the families of our staff, without whose patience, understanding and support our staff would not have been able to achieve what they have...

To David Naylor and the Joint Venture Partners who have guided and directed the growth and progress of the company and whose support and assistance have helped Chan & Naylor develop into a national firm...

This legacy is a reminder of the sacrifices and dedication of all the men and women above who have given their absolute all to make Chan & Naylor a truly great company that they can all be so proud of.

I thank you all.

# Disclaimer

The material in this publication is of a general nature, and neither purports nor intends to be advice. Readers should not act on the basis of any matter in this publication without taking professional advice from a business consultant , tax agent or licensed financial planner, with due regard to their own particular circumstances. The Authors and publisher expressly disclaim all and any liability to any person, whether a purchaser of this publication or not, in respect of anything and of the conse- quences of anything done or omitted to be done by any such person in reliance, whether whole or partial, upon the whole or any part of the contents of this publication.

# Contents

# Testimonials

### *HERE'S WHAT PEOPLE HAVE SAID ABOUT THE BOOK*

"Having successfully started, run and sold several small businesses, we have come to realise the importance of surrounding yourself with a team of successful people who have achieved what you wish to achieve. Having been a client of Chan and Naylor for the past 6 years, David, Ed and the Chan & Naylor team are an integral part of our mastermind group. Without their knowledge, guidance and advice, our journey would have been slow and full of unnecessary mistakes. This book is a must read for anyone who has a business or is wanting to start a business."

*—Lee Sutherland and Justin Christopher.*

When I joined Chan & Naylor as a joint venture partner, I inherited an experienced team with a strong client centric culture and sound procedures built on the basis of Ed and Dave's concepts described in this book. The continued success of this business is a testament to the fact that this is not just about theory but practical, hands-on strategies that work and I strongly recommend to those thinking of starting a business or currently working in small business to read this book .

— *Clive Nelson,* Chan and Naylor Parramatta office

I have been privileged to watch Ed Chan and David Naylor grow their business from a very modest small business into a substantial and sustainable one. Both are exceptional entrepreneurs with solid financial backgrounds and both know how to use their knowledge, experience and enthusiasm in the best way possible. Through their accounting practice they have been exposed to many types of businesses and they have absorbed all this knowledge and experience from having front row seats, looking into their clients businesses. Their ideas and teachings are Best Practice!

*Alan Osrin*, Managing Director, Sage Software Australia

As a Joint Venture Partner of Chan & Naylor I was introduced to the Firm culture, strategies, systems and processes outlined in the book. This has definitely resulted in growing my businessmuch faster, more efficiently and much more successfully than I would have otherwise done. This book is not only a great story, but also an invaluable tool for any small business operator.

*Lilian Fisher* — Partner, Chan & Naylor Perth

I have had the privileged of knowing Ed and Dave for almost a decade — initially as a supplier and then as a co-business owner. Over that time I have been very fortunate to hear, observe and practicemany of the strategies and tactics that Ed and Dave have employed and reveal in this book. By implementing the strategies and tactics revealed in this book I have been able to achieve greater financial success and much better outcomes than I would have achieved without adopting them — I wish that this book was available 30 years ago when I was starting out in business! I can highly recommend this book to anyone in business who wants to maximise their success and minimise their risk in the easiest possible way.

*Des Whyte C.A.* — Chairman eknowhow group

"Dave and Ed are those sort of clients that you feel bad to send an invoice to. They are the gentlemen of business and care for their staff, suppliers and customers equally. It is no surprise they run such a successful business when they have passed this ethos to their group. I commend both for their great results as well as their passion for fun and prosperity in their business endeavours and you are in for a great learning adventure when you read this book."

*Gareth Jekel* — CEO Asia Region — Performia International.

"I have been involved with Chan and Naylor for many years in both a professional and personal capacity. Within this time, the focus of both Ed Chan and David Naylor never waivered. They both know what needs to be done and how to get there with the remarkable emphasis always being on the well being of the client. The clients always come first and with this one simple philosophy, the growth of the company was assured. It was easy for Ed and David to know what the clients need as they have been hands on with the clients since the beginning. If you want to grow your businesssuccessfully, then put all of the other books down and read this one. I look forward to the future of Chan and Naylor."

*George Kafantaris* — Director Mosaic Property Management

Over the past decade I have been fortunate to have been involved in a couple of successful start-ups in my business life. Initially, the prospect was pretty daunting but I found that when you have the professional assistance and guidance of people like Ed Chan and David Naylor and the team not only does it take the pressure off, but it enables you to avoid the pitfalls that colleagues seem to have fallen into. This book is a must for anyone considering either starting a new business, or has begun a new business and is struggling with the journey.

*Jeff Jarratt* — MD Jarratt Enterprises.

"I manage a Buyers Agency helping clients find homes and investment properties around Australia. We have been using Chan and Naylor for many years and appreciate their attention to detail, high quality advice and strategic approach to accounting and business advice. As experts in their field, they are very dedicated to minimizing tax and providing a sounding board for important investment and business decisions. They have an excellent business model and their systems and processes are worth emulating. Edand David and are down to earth people but provide very smart advice tailored to your situation. It's great to learn from someone that has walked the business journey with success and is willing to share that knowledge and experience."

*Rich Harvey* — Managing Director, www.propertybuyer.com.au

For over ten years I have the pleasure to work with and watch the Chan & Naylor business. Chan & Naylor have always been at the forefront of innovation in terms of their approach to business and meeting the needs of their clients.

Chan & Naylor are not your traditional accounting firm, they seek out and invest in research that will deliver real benefits for their clients.

They deliver real client outcomes and don't just count the beans. We look forward to working closely with them for the next ten years. This book is a must read for any business owner.

*Mark Flack* — Executive Director, Firstfolio Limited

"Working with Ed and Dave provided many insights into what it takes to build a successful business. This book condenses many of those insights that can only be realised after years of experience. So do yourself a favour, buy it and read it."

*Tony Melvin* — Author

# Recommended Reference Material

- *The E Myth* by Michael Gerber
- *The 7 Habits of Highly Effective People* by Dr StephenRCovey
- *How to Win Friends and Influence People* by Dale Carnegie
- *Built to Last* by James C. Collins, Jerry I. Porras
- *McDonalds: Behind the Arches* by John F Love
- *Living the 80/20 Way* by Richard Koch
- *Who Moved My Cheese* by Spencer Johnson
- *Good to Great* by Jim Collins
- *How to Legally Reduce Your Tax* by Ed Chan and Tony Melvin
- *How to Buy Property with your Superannuation Fund* by Ed Chan and Tony Melvin
- *How to achieve Wealth for Life Through Property Investing* by Ed Chan and Tony Melvin
- *Tuesdays With Morrie* Mitch Albom

# Part 1
# Humble Beginnings

*"While most are dreaming of success, Winners wake up and work hard to achieve it."*

**—Anonymous**

# FOREWORD

We are Ed Chan and David Naylor, and we began our partnership more than 20 years ago in a small office in Oatlands, Western Sydney. We had one receptionist and the annual turnover of our business was around $50,000. Yes, you could say they were very humble beginnings.

Young, naive and enthusiastic, we began a journey into the unknown by trying to create a thriving and successful small business with little more to offer than energy, eagerness and a good attitude.

Little did we realise back then, in 1990, what we would achieve over the next two decades — nor did we understand the challenges we would face!

The process involved every human emotion possible, from frustration, pain, hopelessness and exhaustion through to satisfaction, success and elation.

Today, the Chan & Naylor group is a prominent national brand in the Australian accounting and professional services landscape. We have eight offices nationwide and more than 100 team members, with an annual turnover in excess of $14 million. We certainly have come a long way!

Through trial and error over the past 20 years, we have developed a range of techniques and skills that have helped us to establish and nurture around 16 associated businesses. And this is the purpose of our book: to show you what we've learnt, how we have overcome the obstacles we've faced, and how we've become successful.

There are many businesses throughout the country that boast fantastic products or services, and they have profitable prospects, but they fail because the business owner doesn't have the right skill set to manage the business effectively and efficiently.

Unfortunately, the collapse of a small business can have far- reaching consequences in society. Not only can it meanbankruptcy, a loss of assets for the owner and financial impacts on innocent creditors, but it can also lead to a breakdown of the family unit and even the loss of life.

Our journey to this point has not always been smooth sailing

there have been plenty of bumps along the way — but in this book, we hope to demonstrate to you how you can benefit from our learnings and use the successful strategies that we've developed in your own small business. We hope to inspire small business owners who dream of success, and show you that triumph is possible.

This book is for people who are thinking of starting a business, and for those who are currently working in their own business — and even for those people who are simply looking for inspiration.

The beauty of this book is that it has value to both small and large businesses, as we have experienced all of the business cycles —including good times and bad. We have applied all of the principles and strategies outlined in this book ourselves so we have genuinely walked the walk.

As a result, this book is not just about theory, and it's not a glossy highlight of our success. It is about practical, proven, tried and tested strategies that can help small business owners achieve their dreams of creating businesses that provide the lifestyles they desire and acquire the ultimate prize: choice.

We hope that this book goes some way towards assisting you on your journey as you create that dream. Good luck!

## 1. ABOUT THE AUTHORS

### *EDWARD CHAN*

I live in Sydney with my wife Donna and our three children Amy, Ryan and Mitchell.

Born in Rabaul in Papua New Guinea in June 1959 — which was part of Australia until granted independence in 1975 — I am a second generation Australian. My father was also born in Papua New Guinea.

My mother was born in China and was separated from her father at birth due to the White Australia Policy in the late 1930s. She did not see nor meet her father until she was nine years old, when she and her mother (my grandmother) joined her father (my grandfather) in Sydney after the abolition of the policy. Their family eventually moved to Papua New Guinea, where she met and married my father, her life-long husband and partner.

My father owned a business in Rabaul but my parents saw the need to provide me with a solid education, so they sent me to boarding school at Holy Cross College Ryde, Sydney, and later to St. Joseph's College in Hunters Hill, Sydney. There, I enjoyed and achieved high results in many sports, including rugby, basketball and squash.

After high school I went on to attend the University of Technology where I completed a Bachelor of Business, majoring in Accounting. Upon graduation I was employed by a large accounting group, PKF, and later by various smaller chartered accounting firms, before I embarked on a short stint in a commercial firm.

I first met David in the early 1980's when we were both working in a small chartered accountancy practice — but more on that later.

Throughout this time, as I was honing my skills and developing my career, I would regularly get asked to prepare tax returns and accounts for friends and family members, which I would attend to in the evenings after knocking off from my full-time job.

This sideline work grew to the point where I was no longer able to manage both my regular job and the extra work, so I was forced to make a decision.

I felt like I needed some business experience, so I left my job and purchased a small distribution business. Over a period of four years, I grew this business from an annual turnover of $60,000 to over $3.5 million. It was financially successful but I was itching to return to accountancy and eventually sold the business.

With the proceeds of the sale, I bought a house with a mortgage and started a family, which meant my wife's wages ceased as she became a full-time mum.

I approached David about the possibility of launching an accountancy firm together and, on the 1st July 1990, that idea became a reality. With a small amount of savings and an eagerness to succeed, we joined to establish Chan & Naylor.

Although this was the official date that Chan & Naylor was incorporated, it really began in the mid-1980s when Dave first took over my small parcel of clients while I focused on building my distribution business. So, Chan & Naylor has really been around, one way or another, for over 25 years.

When we first launched the business, I remember saying to David that we should give ourselves two years to get going, because we only had enough savings between us to last that long. If we couldn't earn a living by that stage, then we would pack it all in and find another job.

Keep in mind it was 1990, when many businesses were experiencing difficulties and the economy was in a slight recession. But my feeling was, if we can survive this period, we can survive anything.

We had set a budget for ourselves to generate $100,000 in fees by 30th June 1991. We achieved this by 31st December 1990 — a full six months earlier than we had planned. We had no money for advertising, so the business had grown simply by word of mouth.

We had clients coming to us saying things like, "There is nothing wrong with my current accountant, but you were so highly recommended, I just had to come over and see what all the fusswas about..."

The business grew at a tremendous rate due to great service and creative strategies. However, there were many challenges ahead. You will read all about the difficulties we faced — and how we overcame them — in the coming pages.

In 2007, I made the decision to retire from the day-to-day operations of Chan & Naylor and I now hold the position of non- executive chairman. I continue to speak at seminars and act, along with David, as the public 'face' of the business.

I am a regular presenter of tax and property seminars throughout Australia and South East Asia, and in this capacity I have presented to over 50,000 people over the last few years. On behalf of the Institute of Chartered Accountants, the National Institute of Accountants, Sage Handisoft and various other organisations, I have delivered Best Practice seminars throughout Australia to over 5,000 accountants, showing them how to grow and run their accountancy practices.

Since 2007, I have had the time to assist the Chan & Naylor group with strategic advice at a Board level. I write books and articles for various journals and magazines, contribute to the Chan & Naylor newsletter and spend time working on my personal property investments. I have co-authored three best-selling books — *Wealth for Life Through Property Investing, How to Legally Reduce Your Tax* and *How to Buy Property with Your Super Money* — and I anticipate a few more to come.

I am so proud of Chan & Naylor's journey, from its humble beginnings to its current position as *BRW*'s 40th Largest Accountancy Firm in Australia, and I couldn't be more pleased with our success. Chan & Naylor won the coveted *BRW* Fastest Growing Accountancy Firm for two consecutive years and I'm extremely excited about where the business is planning to go from here.

I am also particularly proud of the team that has joined the Chan & Naylor group, from those who sit at the Board level of Chan & Naylor Australia — David Naylor, Ken Raiss and Managing Director Sal Carerro — to those who hold positions as joint venture partners in our offices around Australia.

The uniqueness of Chan & Naylor is that, as a 'one-stop shop', our various offices and partnerships around Australia are run and managed by people who have an equity interest in their business. In other words, they are not simply employees. They have a financial interest in providing exceptional service because they are co-owners of the business and they have a real passion for helping clients create and retain their wealth.

The Chan & Naylor brand represents Quality and I couldn't be more proud. It is a brand that upholds the highest levels of honesty and integrity and is recognised around Australia not only by our clients, but also by our peers.

I believe that Chan & Naylor's future is very bright indeed.

## DAVID NAYLOR

I live with my wife Dianne and our two boys Ben and Jordan in the very same neighbourhood in which I grew up.

The eldest son of four children, I was born in March 1961. I had a happy childhood, growing up in the local streets and parks on the lower north shore of Sydney.

As a young boy, I had a great passion for sport, excelling in cricket in the summer months and football in winter, with just enough time to take a breath in between.

Leadership qualities began to emerge in these early days, as I was routinely selected as the leader of sporting teams. I quickly began to understand the principles of leading by example and how to get the best out of others.

Sport has had a great influence in my life and I believe that many of the interpersonal and management skills I apply in the business world today were in fact developed on the sporting field. There is an inspirational quote that inspires me each morning when I am feeling less energetic to face the challenges ahead.

> *"When you're not practicing, remember that someone somewhere is practicing and when you meet him he will win"*
>
> — **Ed Macauley**

Team sports highlight all that is required to be a successful manager, employee and/or employer, such as:

1. Working together to achieve a goal and developing a team culture
2. Getting the best performance from the people around you
3. Maintaining fitness to perform at your peak
4. Working closely with teammates to achieve common goals
5. Working within a system to achieve goals
6. Rewarding over-performers
7. Assisting under-performers to reach their potential
8. Accepting defeat and working hard to do better next time
9. Celebrating wins

10. Understanding your strengths and accepting your weaknesses, and then committing to work on these

11. Continuing to learn and developing your skill set with three simple words: practice, practice, practice

12. Knowing there is no replacement for good old hard work and attitude

My drive and self-motivation was evident at a very young age. In those early days, I would spend many a day picking oranges and knocking on doors after school selling the fruit that I had collected. My father was a property developer — hence my passion for property — and my mother looked after my siblings and I in between part-time work. Together, my parents worked very hard in order to provide all of us with the best gift possible, a good education.

I attended St Patrick's College at Strathfield in New South Wales at the age of 10, but I am the first to admit that I was not a great student. Sitting in a classroom for seven hours a day was like being a lion in a cage; my mind wandered to the sporting fields and most days I could not wait until the bell went so that I could clamber on the bus and go down to the local park to play cricket or soccer with my mates.

In my later years of schooling, I did begin to enjoy practical subjects such as English, History and Economics.

Throughout my entire schooling life, however, I always displayed good work ethic. During school holidays, I worked. From selling oranges door-to-door to working in a process line in a cannery, to delivering freight, to being a bricklayer's labourer, I would do almost anything to earn a dollar. Better still, I knew the value in saving it.

In my last year or two of school, my main focus was to get out into the workforce, as I wanted to roll up my sleeves, get amongst it and commence my working life.

Like many school-leavers in the late 1970s who wanted to start their professional life, I turned to the banking industry. The banks offered a solid career path and I knew I had one undeniable skill: determination. If I focused on something that I really wanted, I would stop at nothing to achieve that goal.

I also realised that along with my passion for sport, I had a desire to create wealth. I knew even then that I wanted to be in business, but it was not yet clear to me which direction I would take. I joined the CBC (now the NAB) in 1979, as it seemed the natural progression to get into business and finance.

Here, I progressed from the role of junior ledger clerk to the number one teller of the Balmain branch in Sydney within two years. By then, I was handling large sums of money. The only problem was, it belonged to other people!

This is where my journey really kicked into gear, as I knew that in dealing with money, finance and people, I was on the right bus — I just wasn't in the right seat. I really wanted to be in a position where I could help people and consult with them directly about their finances and business.

After making this decision, I left the bank to further my education. All up I took three years out of my working life to attain the relevant tertiary qualifications. To earn money, I worked as a builder's labourer during the holidays and on days off.

Once I had completed my studies in 1985, I got my first 'real job' in accounting at a small chartered accounting firm in my local area. I was hired by John Fenton and Ted Brailey of Brailey and Fenton Accountants, and I was very grateful to these gentlemen for giving me my first break in the field. In fact, all I wanted to do is pay them back for showing faith in me as their employee.

I have to admit that at first, I wasn't sure what I was getting myself into. I spent many hours thinking, what do I do? How do I do it? Like everyone starting out in the career I had shortcomings in my lack of accounting experience, but I persevered.

Slowly but surely, things improved. What I lacked in experience I made up in sheer hard work and determination. Once, I worked 24 hours straight — on Christmas Eve, no less — to meet a deadline. I think this attitude and commitment meant that my employers sometimes overlooked my lack of experience and kept me on, so it was another lesson learnt. Attitude is critical.

It was in the mid-1980s that I met Ed and the seeds for Chan & Naylor were first sewn. That story plays out in the following pages.

By 2007, Ed and I had built the business to a point where we felt it could run on a day-to-day basis without us working as accountants. Therefore, I retired from my general practice role and held the position of managing director of the national group for 12 months, before I moved to a more strategic role as a member of the Board.

I continue to assist the Chan & Naylor group with strategic advice at a Board level and, together with Ed, represent the business in the media and write articles for various publications. I also sit on a number of other Boards, providing strategic direction.

In recent years, Ed and I have branched out to co-found EknowhowAccounting Pty Ltd, a web-based intranet and website solution for accountancy firms, which now boasts over 800 clients.

We have also both assisted in the Post Graduate MBA Course offered by the University of Queensland, where Chan & Naylor was used as the benchmark firm. This has since become part of the Certified Practicing Accountant (CPA) program studied by thousands of students.

I am truly proud of the success that Chan & Naylor has achieved, and I believe that the best is yet to come. My ambition is to leave a legacy in the professional services industry that will continue well beyond my lifetime.

## ED & DAVID MEET — THE FIRE IS LIT

### *IN DAVID'S WORDS...*

The year was 1986, and Brailey and Fenton Accountants was growing at quite a pace. New team members were arriving every other week, but I remember the arrival of one young man in particular. How could I forget, when the person in question walked right up to my desk, extended his hand and confidently introduced himself? "Hello, my name is Ed. Ed Chan," he said. Little did either of us realise that this shake of the hand would be the start of an incredible journey.

From very early on, it was quite clear that Ed was a leader.He was employed as my client manager/supervisor and he took on this role with his trademark enthusiasm.

Ed was never one to let life roll by. If things needed to be changed, he would speak up. If his staff were being treated unfairly, he would make it known. He was a man of principles and he stood by them, rightly or wrongly, which sometimes meant that he ruffled a few feathers and egos.

For some reason, our personalities seemed to gel.

As our working relationship and friendship evolved, we did not realise that we were actually cultivating the very beginning of Chan & Naylor.

One day, Ed came to me and announced that he was leaving the firm. By this point we had developed a strong friendship, so Ed offered me a small group of his relatives and friends as clients to manage on the side. I was thrilled; I already had quite a few contacts of my own and with Ed's new clients, I had a decent little portfolio. And so off Ed went into the commercial accounting world, while I remained with the firm and managed a small group ofpersonal clients on the side. Funnily enough, the majority are still Chan & Naylor clients today!

Initially, I began servicing these clients after-hours. But my portfolio began to grow through word-of-mouth referrals and within a short while a decision had to be made: should I keep doing what I had been doing, working long hours on my day job and working at night with my personal clients or should I leave the safety and security of full-time employment to start my own business?

I was debating this choice over and over in my head, although I knew there was really only one option. I was still on the bus and a few more seats were available. It was time to throw my hat in the ring as a small business owner.

So I too said goodbye to the security of full-time employment and set up my home office in the back room of my parents' home. I bought a computer, a printer, a desk and a chair, and sat back and thought, hooray, I'm free! How naïve I was. I had no idea that I was about to create a monster.

For a year or so, I serviced clients from my parents' house, but I knew I needed to grow the business and create a steady income. One day I answered an ad in the newspaper that called for the contract services of an accountant, and I saw this as a great opportunity to supplement my meagre income and grow the business at the same time.

The office was in a small, leafy suburb of Western Sydney called Oatlands. When I first walked through those doors, I had no way of knowing that the office would eventually become the headquarters for Chan & Naylor, and that both Ed and I would spend the next 15 years growing a business within those four walls. We even ended up owning the building, which was another great business decision, but we'll get to that later!

Alan Litto was the accountant who had placed the ad. He was bursting at the seams, working hour upon hour trying to hold things together and he desperately needed some help. When I partnered with Alan, it was a perfect solution for both of us: Alan had the assistance he needed and I had a regular income stream to supplement my cash flow, along with a commercial office from which to service my own clients.

While all of this was going on, Ed and I had kept in touch, as I was still servicing Ed's friends and relatives as clients. In 1990, I received a phone call from Ed that would change everything...

Ed: "Hi Dave, it's Ed here. How are things?" David: "Good, can't complain — and you?"

Ed: "Fine, thanks. Hey, how about we get together and form a business?"

David: "Umm... mate, I only have about $50,000 worth of fees. How will that fund both of our wages and the costs of running a business?"

Ed: "I don't know." Silence.

David: "What the heck! Nothing ventured, nothing gained. Come on board for the ride... I think this bus is heading in the right direction, and there is plenty of room..."

I had heard of the term 'synergy', but until that point I had not seen it in action. But there it was, a perfect partnership where 1 + 1 = 3... or, in our case, much, much more.

# PART 2
# Changing Your Mindset

*"I'd rather attempt to do something great and fail, than to attempt to do nothing and succeed."*

**Robert Schuller**

When we started out, we didn't have much going for us other than a strong desire for success and a small portfolio of clients. Today, our business boasts multi-million dollar annual profits. The road from point A to point B certainly wasn't smooth, but we're willing to share the lessons and experiences we have had along the way.

Essentially, the purpose of writing this book is two-fold. Firstly, we both understand the pain, the frustration and the helplessness that small business owners experience on a day-to-day basis when running and growing their businesses.

Who do you turn to for help? Where do you go when you feel trapped and suffocated by this monster that you've created? Where has your life gone — and where is it going?!

If you feel this way, hopefully this book can help answer some of these questions and give you some guidance and direction — or, at the very least, offer comfort in the knowledge that we've been there and done that, and have come through the other side.

What gives us the right to talk to you about this? Well, we've experienced these feelings first-hand, so all of the information contained in this book is based on twenty five years of practical experience. All of our principles have been tested and proven — they're not just thoughts or ideas, but theory that we've put into practice.

Our aim is to help you help yourself. Sometimes the solutions we suggest are not the obvious answers, and we hope that by outlining these theories in practical terms, it will help you 'see the light' so you can take control of your business and your life.

The second reason we wrote this book is that the Chan & Naylor brand and business model has expanded across Australia, so we felt the need to create a 'Bible' about the business.

The purpose of this is to assist our joint venture partners, clients and our growing number of team members to understand the origins, values and culture of our organisation. This book enables us to leverage our knowledge and help induct new people into our growing family.

At the same time, this book will provide a framework that any business owner can use, by taking some or all of the fundamentals expressed throughout these pages and applying them to their own business.

## THE FUNDAMENTALS OF BUSINESS

One of the most important things that we've learnt throughout the course of growing our business is the role that mindset plays.

Before we even get to that, though, we must explain the first and most fundamental principle of business ownership. Understanding this is crucial to the success of your business, and it's important that you come to grips with this before you even begin.

You may be the best mechanic, accountant, dentist, plumber or doctor in your local area.

You may be the brightest engineer or the most successful real estate agent.

But just because you excel in your chosen field, that doesn't necessarily mean you'll be the best business owner or operator.

The skills you've developed through obtaining your qualification and becoming good at your job are completely different to the skills you need to become successful in the business world.

Not only are these skills very different, but it's also crucial to recognise that you may not have the right skill-set you need to successfully own and operate a business. The most successful business owners are those who recognise their own strengths and weaknesses, and who hire complementary skills to combat this, rather than trying to do everything themselves.

The statistics are devastating. They indicate that 80% of small businesses fail within the first five years of operation, and of the 20% of those businesses that survive, 80% fail within the next five years.

This illustrates how important it is to find the right seat on the bus; it's absolutely paramount to ensuring that your business is a success.

Only around 4% of businesses survive beyond the initial 10-year period, and the survival of your business beyond that 10- year period depends on this simple premise: that as the owner, you progress from working **in** the business to working **on** the business.

For instance, you may need to progress from being a person **doing** the actual work — a technician — to becoming a person who's involved in **managing** the work. If you can't or don't hire the technicians to do the work — so that you can get on with managing the business workflow, clients and your systems — then you may join the growing list of businesses which fail.

As most small business people are trained as technicians in their respective line of business, it's a challenge to shift their focus in this way — but it is critical if you want to succeed.

In his book *E-Myth*, Michael Gerber describes the business life cycle as follows. Most businesses fail in the second period of this business cycle.

| **Cycle** | **Action** | **Timeframe** |
|---|---|---|
| 1. Infancy — The Doing Cycle | Owner completes the technical work of the business. | 0-5 years |
| 2.Adolescence — The People Management Cycle | Owner hires people and learns to manage other people doing the work rather than doing the work themselves. | 5-10 years |
| 3. Maturity — The Systems Development Cycle | Owner creates a business that works without the owner. This only happens with the appropriate systems and the right mix of people and culture. | 10 years beyond |

The ultimate goal is to create a business that works so that the owner doesn't have to.

Therefore, the idea is to develop a business that gives the owner/s a sustainable cash flow and dividend, and brings enjoyment to their lives rather than despair. This is a business that works **without** the owner. Instead, the owner's role should be simply to ensure that the systems are working and the business is getting the best out of its people.

To achieve this, the first thing that needs to change is the owner's way of looking at the business, because the business won't change unless the owner changes. As the saying goes, the definition of insanity is **expecting a different result, but doing things the same way** — but nothing will ever change if nothing changes.

## YOUR INNER CONTROL FREAK

By changing the way you think about the business, you begin a new journey.

In order to create a business that runs without you working in it, the question you need to ask is: how would this get done if I weren't here to do it?

You have to open your mind and accept change, because what you learnt at school, university or any other institution generally doesn't prepare you for running your own business.

You may even have to go back to school to re-educate and up-skill yourself, and learn how to become a manager and a leader. The skills required to run your own business and manage and lead people can be far more complex than those skills required to actually do the work.

Getting two, four, 10 or 100 people doing what you used to do effectively and efficiently is one of the most difficult trades you'll ever have to learn. However, if you can master this skill, it will create tremendous leverage — and, all of a sudden, running your own business will bring you joy, not despair.

When a client tells us that they do not want to grow their business, it's generally because they associate growth with pain. But in reality, who would not want growth — and the wealth that comes with it — if they knew they could do it painlessly and easily.

In this book, we will share concepts, ideas and strategies to demonstrate exactly how you can grow your business without the pain, effort and stress that most people associate with growing a business.

In order to begin this process, you must first recognise that you can't do everything all by yourself. Many business owners idly plough on regardless, using brute strength to keep the wheels turning. They put in the extra hours to keep the whole business afloat. But because they want control and they're scared to let go, they refuse to delegate important tasks to other team members. We call these people **control freaks**.

A typical comment from a control freak is, "If you want something done properly, you simply have to do it yourself." But really what these people are saying is that they can't trust someone else to do the work, because those people don't show the same attention to detail. They're afraid that these people will make mistakes that will prompt the client or customer to leave the business, or they're simply not comfortable letting go.

In these scenarios, the business is usually not functioning as a business should. There are no systems or procedures in place, and generally there has been little investment in training.

Why? Because these types of business owners view time spent training team members or developing systems as a **cost** rather than an **investment** in building their business.

Therein lies the problem. What's required is a change of mindset, which is easier said than done — but isn't it better to have someone else do 80% for you, rather than you having to contribute the full 100%?

This can be a very difficult concept for some people to accept, and it usually comes down to a fear of failure. Unless you can get over this feeling of having control over every single aspect of your business, then you will never be in a position to truly grow, prosper and enjoy the financial freedom that a successful business can deliver.

Let's consider the costs of doing business another way. If you want to generate passive income from property rental yields and share dividends, then you must invest in a property or the share market.

In a similar vein, if you want your business to work autonomously while paying you dividends, then you must be prepared to invest back into your own business. In this case, the investment that is required involves training your staff, implementing systems and leveraging your efforts through these channels.

When Chan & Naylor was first starting out, for a period of several years, we took very little money out of the firm for personal use and kept re-investing back into the business. When associates around us were withdrawing large sums from their own businesses and living a high life, we maintained low-key lifestyles and kept our eye on the bigger picture.

We adopted a long-term view because we knew that ultimately, our goal was to create a business that worked so that we didn't have to. That investment has well and truly paid off: today, we work because we want to and not because we have to. We enjoy a passive income stream and have the gift of choice in terms of how we spend our days — and, best of all, the vision that we had for Chan & Naylor has been realised.

## THE REAL MEANING OF 'BALANCE SHEET' VS. 'PROFIT & LOSS'

During the course of the book, we'll use and explain a number of terms that we apply in the day-to-day culture of Chan & Naylor. These work very well and you'll need to understand these terms in order to apply them in your own business. Two important terms are as follows:

**Balance Sheet:** The Balance Sheet is like a window into your business. It tells you what the net worth of your business is and shows all of your Assets and Liabilities. When you buy equipment or office furniture, it goes into the Asset column of your Balance Sheet. Money in the bank account or an investment is also an Asset in your Balance Sheet. If you owe money to a bank or lender, this appears as a Liability. The net result of your Assets less your Liabilities equals your business's Net Worth.

**Profit & loss:** The Profit & Loss of a business is a recording of all the Income (sales), less the Expenses incurred to generate these sales for a given financial period. For example, an Expense might be the rent paid for the use of premises, wages paid to staff or telephone costs. The net result of Income exceeding Expenses is called a Profit. If your Expenses exceed your Income, it's a Loss.

Now that you have a basic understanding of the Balance Sheet and Profit & Loss, let's discuss how most business owners tend to misunderstand the definitions above. It's important to change this mindset because to be successful, you need to view these from a different perspective.

When we were growing our business, we initially saw hiring a new team member as an expense, which fell into our Profit & Loss statement. In other words, we thought the more people we hire, the higher our costs, and the lower our profits will be at the end of the day.

However, we soon realised that we were looking at it from the wrong perspective. If you think about it, hiring and training a new person enables more income to be generated, which allows the business to grow and the business owners to leverage their time.

As an example, if it costs $70,000 per year to employ and train a new staff member and cover fixed costs, and that employee generates or services $100,000 worth of new business annually, then profits would increase by $30,000 every financial year.

In actual fact, a new staff member is an investment and should come under the Asset side of the Balance Sheet. Once we got our mind around this concept, we started to view things differently.

We also began to realise that the amount of money we spent on educating and training ourselves to become better managers, and educating and training our staff, was a wise investment.

Initially, we saw this as a cost on the Profit & Loss statement and we were reluctant to put time and money into training and education. However once we saw this as an investment in our Balance Sheet, it literally changed our lives.

Developing systems and procedures is also a Balance Sheet item. Ditto for spending money on the right IT system. Once we got our mind around these definitions, we started to question every expense. Is this a Balance Sheet investment, which is adding value to our business, or Profit & Loss cost?

With this thought process, we allowed ourselves to re-invest in the business and it became easier to make decisions. It was all a matter of shifting our mindset. We'll be referring to these definitions throughout the book to help you understand how these principles apply in a practical setting.

## YOUR MENTORS

In order to be an effective and efficient manager and business owner, you need to up-skill and re-invest in yourself via education and training.

There are plenty of books that can assist you, including many that we mention throughout this book (see the summary at the front). These publications have been instrumental in our own personal development and business growth, and we highly recommend that you read them.

However, every successful businessperson knows that they can't achieve what they want by themselves. Just as elite sportspeople require coaches and facilitators to ensure they reach their full potential, you as a business owner must surround yourself with successful people in their respective fields. You should always pay for good advice, as this is an investment (Balance Sheet) and not an expense (Profit & Loss).

To evaluate the people you work with, there is one proviso that we always recommend. Start by asking your advisor if they've ever done it for themselves. There's no substitute for first-hand experience, and if they've been there and done that, they're much more likely to be able to offer quality advice.

Don't feel inadequate by asking for help; instead, leverage off people and learn from them. Most of all, make sure you implement what you've learnt. We strongly believe that 10% of the result is achieved by gaining knowledge and education, and 90% of the result is putting it into practice.

# PART 3
# The Business Life Cycle

The Chan & Naylor business was officially incorporated on 1st July 1990. Prior to this, Ed had been running his own business and David had been managing a small portfolio of accounting clients in a small office in Oatlands, Western Sydney.

We both experienced all of the normal emotions associated with making the decision to start a business. We ran through many concerns together, such as:

1. Will we be able to generate enough money to pay our salaries?
2. How will we generate new business?
3. Can we pay the rent and expenses on an ongoing basis?

At the same time, we experienced the dual feelings of excitement (because we were **free from constraints** of normal full-time employment) and concern (because we were **leaving the security** of normal full-time employment).

Somewhat naively, we jumped straight into this thing we called a business. We didn't have much of a business plan and we certainly had no understanding of business life cycles. We basically hung the shingle on the door and announced that we were open for business.

Even though the industry you're in or product that you produce may be different to accountancy, you will find that the fundamental principles that drive success are the same across all businesses — so let us share our experience with you.

## STAGE ONE: DOING

People start their own business for many different reasons. Some want to earn more money. Others don't want a boss to report to. Many like the idea that they go to work to build something for themselves, while others like the freedom and flexibility that it can provide.

Then there are those people who go into business for completely the wrong reasons. An example of this is someone who is running away from a job they hate. They feel like they're ready for a different experience, but the downside — if the business fails — can be potentially devastating, financially and emotionally.

We launched our business because we wanted freedom. We were young and enthusiastic, and the business grew quite quickly through hard work and the delivery of exemplary personal service to our clients. We started to get word-of-mouth referrals from clients because of this commitment to quality and service, and our workload grew quite quickly as a result.

Initially, the team consisted of a young receptionist and us. Between the three of us, we managed the day-to-day operations of the business, including banking, answering the phone, washing up, cleaning the office and much, much more. We were happy with this arrangement as the business was growing, money was coming in and we felt that things were progressing well.

How then, within just a few short years, did everything go pear-shaped?

Business was good. Cash flow was okay. New business was pouring in. So what was the problem?

This business that we had established in order to give us freedom and create more free time and flexibility for us to enjoy our lives — well, it had done the exact opposite. Essentially, we had created a monster.

This business that we created to give us life, was actually taking life from us.

Because of our enthusiasm to grow this business, we would take on any and all newcomers as clients. Basically, anyone who could breathe could become a client, regardless of the fact that our workloads were already over capacity.

Because we were doing such a great job and providing such high quality individual service and attention, we were also generating referrals from family, friends and existing clients faster than we could keep up with them. In order to maintain the level of work we were bringing in, we had to work longer hours. Much longer hours. In fact, we were working around 15 hours per day, six to seven days per week, just to get the work done.

And that's when we started to drop the ball.

The situation was completely unsustainable and our work began to suffer. When we started to receive complaints, we realised that we had reached full capacity — but we didn't know what to do about it.

We were physically drained, which meant that we viewed the client as adding to our pain. This was no fault of the client, but was a symptom of the problem: an ever-increasing workload.

Consequently, dealing with our clients then became a chore rather than a pleasant experience. When the phone rang with a prospective new client, rather than eagerly accepting the call and trying to sell them our services with enthusiasm, we were deflated. We saw them as adding more work to our already stretched workload, and it was cultivating a negative attitude.

It's an attitude that you may have received as a customer over the years. You enter a store and the person behind the counter doesn't need to say a word, because you can see it in their face: "Oh no, here comes another customer..."

It was a terrible attitude and we weren't enjoying life. On a day-to-day basis, liaising with clients and churning through work was becoming a chore, rather than being a service that we enjoyed providing.

This wasn't meant to be!

The whole point of starting our own business was to escape the grind of the 9–5 day working for someone else so that we could create working conditions that gave us more flexibility and freedom.

Furthermore, working as accountants — our chosen professional field — was actually something that we both enjoyed. Or, at least, we had enjoyed up until this point.

What happened next gave us the wake-up call we needed. We started to lose clients.

We also formed bad habits with the clients we had retained, such as being available on weekends and after-hours. Needless to say, this began to affect not just our professional capabilities, but also our personal lives.

Our family members were being neglected because of our long working hours, and even when we did spend time together, we were often on the phone to clients anyway.

We realised that we were spinning out of control, so we made that quantum leap. We knew what we needed: help. Professional, expert help — and fast.

***BUSINESS LIFE CYCLE***

**STAGE 1**
**DOING**

**Begin**
- Excited
- Take any new Client/ Customer
- A little apprehensive
- Do everything yourself:
- do the work, washing plates, making coffee, answering phones etc.
- Starts slowly at the beginning

GROWTH

- Deliver extras such as: work Saturdays, give home phone numbers etc
- Now extras become standards
- Client enjoy personal attention
- Experience tremendous growth
- Workload Increases

HIT WALL

## SO WHAT NOW? A PARADIGM SHIFT

Again, somewhat naively, we thought that simply hiring a person to do the excess work that we couldn't handle would provide the right answer. How wrong we were!

Adding another accountant to our team simply introduced new problems, frustrations and challenges. Back then, we weren't equipped with the knowledge and skills we have now regarding staff recruitment and retention, so we were effectively introducinga solution that brought with it a whole new set of problems.

We were determined to find the right solution but, to be completely honest, we had no idea where to look.

So we looked at selling the business.

We considered selling off the smaller clients so we could concentrate on our larger, more profitable clients.

We thought about bringing in new partners.

We even discussed increasing fees as a strategy to stem the flow of too much new work coming through the door and give us the time to concentrate on our existing client base.

### *SELLING*

At the time, within our industry it was becoming more common for accountants to offer additional services, other than the standard compliance work like preparing tax returns.

This included 'business development' type work with clients, as there appeared to be much more money to be made in business development than there was in compliance work

Others in the marketplace, such as financial planners and finance brokers, were earning greater hourly rates than accountants. This prompted many accountants to close up or sell off their compliance practices to become full-time business development practices and/or financial planning businesses.

We considered moving in this new direction but, even back then when things were not entirely clear, we felt that switching our service offering would only provide a quick fix at best. It would simply be addressing the symptoms, rather than fixing the problems, and we knew that **it was not the industry that we were in that was the issue — it was how we were managing our business.**

Over the years we've seen this happen quite a lot, where clients jump from industry to industry. They claim there is "no money" in their current venture, so they try and find fortune in another industry. The fact of the matter is that if they ran their businesses the correct way, they would save themselves a lot of time, energy and money. Instead, they repeat the same problems in another industry and constantly chase that illusive 'big break' that they feel will finally relieve their frustrations and pain and make them wealthy.

So, we knew that if we sold the practice and took the framework of how we were running our business to another industry, within a few years we would be back to the same situation... burnt out and working really long hours, without much to show for it.

We had to find a solution, but that proved to be a challenge, as we didn't really know what the problem was — let alone how to find a solution!

Selling off smaller clients to concentrate on larger clients also didn't fix the problem, because we simply went from being really busy looking after smaller clients to being really busy looking after larger clients.

## ADDING PARTNERS

It is said that an accountancy firm should have around seven or eight staff members per partner, with fees of around $1 million per partner. At this level, profits are created through leverage and not the brute effort of the partners.

On the other hand, if you have fees of $1 million and three partners, that would equate to only $333,000 per partner. This practice wouldn't be considered very successful as the fees are generated by the brute strength of the partners, which is unsustainable. Eventually, the partners will burn out and move on.

At the time, we didn't know these financial guidelines and thought that bringing in new blood in the form of a new partner would be the answer to our prayers.

However, we learnt that bringing in new partners didn't fix the problem, because although they brought with them responsibility, experience and the ability to take a lot of pressure off our plates, they also brought another set of problems. Partners are expensive, and they expect to be paid appropriately for their services. This substantially reduced our own profits, which brought us back to squareone.

## INCREASING FEES

Increasing prices is a strategy that some businesses use to stem the flow of too much new work coming through the door.

The thinking behind this is that demand is so high that you can price your services to meet the market demand. However, this is a strategy that again simply addresses the symptoms rather than fixing the problem.

If you were to adopt this strategy and increase your prices simply because you're unable to run your business efficiently, you're doing the wrong thing by your client and at the end of the day, they won't stand for it. Unless an increase in rates or prices is justified, your clients won't pay inflated prices over the long term and, eventually, they will leave.

## OUR NEXT MOVE

One day we saw an article in *BRW* magazine, which talked about a very successful accountant, John, who was running a very successful practice with a turnover of $2 million.

John wasn't a stranger, but rather someone that Ed had worked with in the past and knew quite well. So, we decided to call him.

We were at our wits' end with the practice and could no longer sustain the long hours. We needed to know what John was doing that allowed him to run a $2 million practice efficiently while we were struggling to run a $200,000 practice.

When Ed dialled John's number, we expected the call to go to voicemail. After all, we knew how much time and effort went into running our business and it was only turning over 10% of the fees that John's firm was generating. Surely, John would be far too busy to take Ed's call.

Instead, Ed was shocked when the receptionist connected him through to John immediately.

"John, I didn't think I would be able to catch you," Ed began. "Well, you're right, I'm not normally in on a Wednesday afternoon," John replied.

*I knew it,* Ed thought. *I was right! He must work enormously long hours...*

"I usually pick my kids up from school on a Wednesday afternoon," John continued, "and then I take the whole of Thursday off to play golf every week. But I came into the office today because I left my golf shoes in the office, and you just happened to catch me."

It was incredible. Here we were, working over 100 hours a week with a practice that was a 10th of the size of John's business, and yet he seemed to have so much more time.

"How on earth do you do it, John?" Ed asked.

"Look, I'm actually running late to pick up my kids from school, but why don't you speak with my secretary so we can line up lunch and I can explain the whole thing to you?"

Ed actually recalls replying, "But I just don't have the time." Thankfully, that appointment went ahead a few weeks later.

Over lunch, Ed explained the frustrations and challenges we were experiencing. Surprisingly, John revealed that he experienced similar issues — the only difference was John's mindset and the way he looked at his business.

We went to work to prepare tax returns, whereas John went to work to build a business that prepared tax returns. These aretwo vastly different tasks.

"Ed, you're doing everything wrong," John explained.

"If I can recommend one thing it's this: read *The E Myth* by Michael Gerber. It will explain everything."

Work was far too busy for Ed to take the time out to go and buy the book, so he asked his wife to pick it up for him.

Then, the book was placed on the table next to his chair, because he was far too busy to read it. Clients were complaining that it was taking too long to get their tax returns completed so we were working over-time. The book sat on the table for four months. We were both taking home files and working through until 1am or 2am in the morning. Finally one night, at around 1am, Ed put his pen down and decided to pick up the book.

Once he began reading he couldn't put the book down and by 6am the following morning, he had finished it. Rather than feeling tired, however, he was excited beyond belief. He couldn't wait to get to work. After reading the book, he finally realised what we were doing wrong. He almost felt that Gerber had written the book specifically about us and our situation!

"David, I've found the answer," Ed beamed as soon as David arrived at work. "It's in this book — I know what we've been doing wrong! Take it and read it, and let's get together when you're finished."

When David began reading the book, he too couldn't put it down.

It's not that the book held all the answers — it's more that the book provided the impetus to start the process of evaluating what we were doing right and wrong.

We realised that we needed to up-skill and re-educate ourselves, because the skills required to **do** the work were one thing, but the skills required to manage **someone else** to do the work was another thing altogether.

We sat down and worked out a plan, starting with writing down what we each wanted our business to achieve and listing our priorities in descending order. Surprisingly, we both had the same goal at the top of our list: to spend more time with our families.

However, to do this we needed to create a business that worked **without** us, not **because** of us. This realisation in itself forever changed our daily purpose at work.

The second item on both of our lists was the level of income we required. In order to create a business that worked without us, we needed to employ competent, qualified staff to do the work and liaise confidently with our clients.

This required us to work backwards. We knew that if we wanted to bring in new employees, we would need to introduce new procedures, systems and infrastructure (such as computers and equipment) to maximise their effectiveness.

We also knew that, to pay for these resources and boost our employee pool, we would need to sustain turnover at a certain level.

Thus, by working backwards, we were able to determine what level of turnover was required for the business to run smoothly and generate sufficient incomes for us to lead the lifestyles we wanted.

It was all a matter of leverage. Let's say, by way of example, we wanted to earn $150,000 each per year. We would need to generate $400,000 in turnover each, as this would allow us to hire two accounting staff members and one administration employee at a cost of around $180,000, plus an extra $70,000 to cover overheads such as rent, utilities and supplies.

Many small business owners simply think that they have to do all the work themselves in order to keep overheads low. The shift we made was in changing the way we ran and perceived our business, and this is the key difference. Instead of going to work to prepare a tax return, we were going to work to build a business that prepared tax returns — and, in the process, we were building a business that worked without us and produce profits that ultimately would generate a passive income stream.

This meant that we could choose to work or not to work, as long as the systems and people within the business were doingwhat they were supposed to be doing, in terms of servicing our clients. This gave us the ultimate freedom — choice — which is the true measure of wealth.

Under this new regime, we were able to spend more time with clients on their strategic matters, while our staff worked on their compliance and operational matters. Strategy is how clients create better businesses and build better investments, and consequently make more money and create more wealth.

By working together in this way, we were able to deliver cost- effective services to our clients. They paid lower fees for things such as bookkeeping, BAS preparation and tax returns, but higher fees for value-adding services such as wealth creation, asset protection and tax management strategies. Our clients found these additional services to be extremely valuable, and the result was win-win.

## STAGE TWO: PEOPLE MANAGEMENT

Back in those early days when we were struggling to wade through our ever-increasing workload, we came up with what we thought was a brilliant solution. We hired someone to help us get through the work.

Phew! We've found the answer. We're saved. Now that we have this new person on board, we can concentrate on other areas of the business and get home to our families on time.

This was our thought process initially but, as we mentioned earlier, we had a lot to learn about people management.

We were great technicians: ask us anything about taxation, our specialised field, and we could answer in a split second.

We were very proud of our skills in this area and the clients loved us for it. But the challenge was to work out how to delegate the work to someone else and get that person to do the work in *exactly the same way* as we did, and to ensure the clients loved this new employee as much as they loved us.

They certainly don't teach the answers to these sorts of questions at university or school. We thought our problems were solved, but all that happened was we created a whole new set of problems that zapped our time and energy.

We started to get complaints from clients and a few clients even left. This was because:

1. There was change

2. The new employee didn't do the work exactly like we had done in the past

3. Mistakes were being made

4. Unfortunately, service levels dropped

Okay, okay, if you want something done right, you have to do it yourself... right? This is the line of thinking that we began to consider.

We started to question our growth and whether we had what it took to run a business in general. After all, we'd come up against a challenge and we thought we had found the answer, but it had blown up in our face. So now where do we go and what do we do?

This was our darkest hour in the business cycle, as and we were desperate for an answer. We discussed a number of options:

1. Sell the business and get out

2. Go back to full-time employment

3. Bring in a new partner

4. Sell the business and get into a new industry

Eventually we realised that all we would be doing is jumping from one set of problems to another set of problems. We also realised that our business had a future, as it was profitable and growing; we just had to work out how to harness that potential and move forward.

After all, every big, successful business had to start somewhere.

How did they do it?

We set about searching for solutions as we were looking for a way to keep the business afloat and thriving, without us having to work 90– 100 hours per week to achieve it. Little did we know at the time that this education and searching process would be the beginning of a great success story.

## BUSINESS LIFE CYCLE

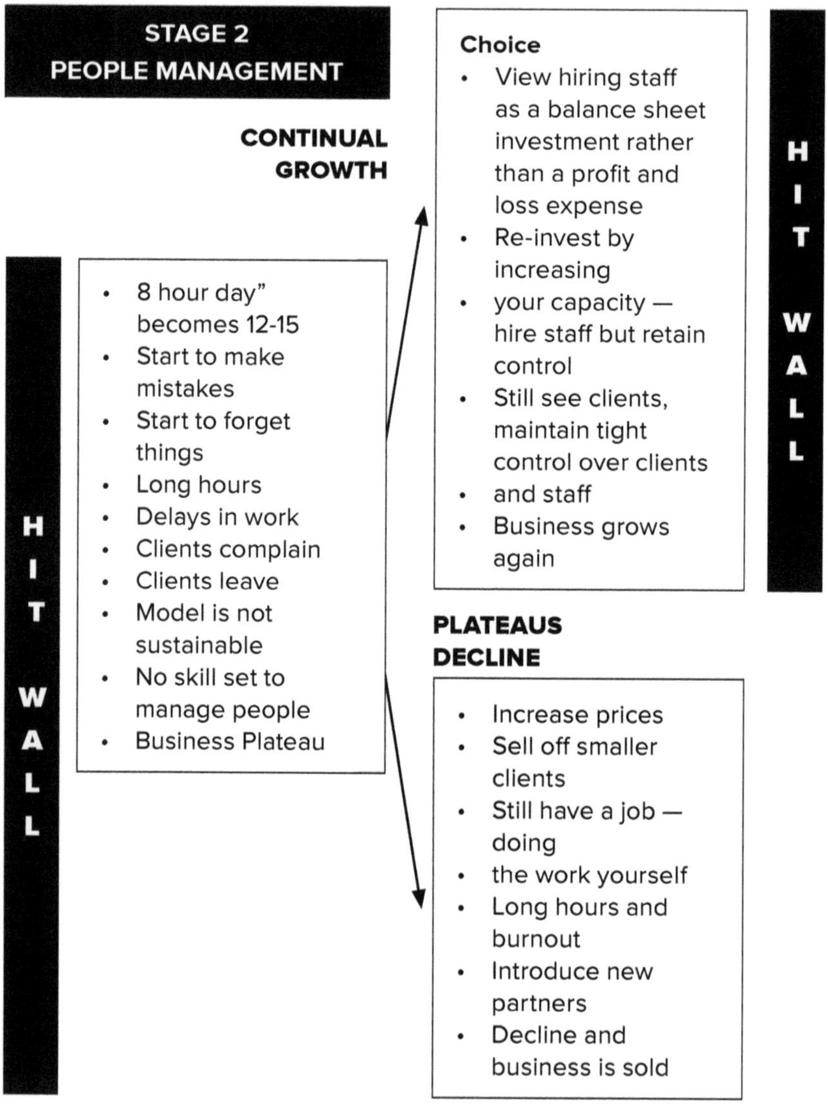

**STAGE 2**
**PEOPLE MANAGEMENT**

HIT WALL

- 8 hour day" becomes 12-15
- Start to make mistakes
- Start to forget things
- Long hours
- Delays in work
- Clients complain
- Clients leave
- Model is not sustainable
- No skill set to manage people
- Business Plateau

**CONTINUAL GROWTH**

**Choice**

- View hiring staff as a balance sheet investment rather than a profit and loss expense
- Re-invest by increasing
- your capacity — hire staff but retain control
- Still see clients, maintain tight control over clients
- and staff
- Business grows again

HIT WALL

**PLATEAUS DECLINE**

- Increase prices
- Sell off smaller clients
- Still have a job — doing
- the work yourself
- Long hours and burnout
- Introduce new partners
- Decline and business is sold

## STAGE THREE: SYSTEMS

As accountants, shifting the paradigm was not an easy journey. After years of being technicians and filling out timesheets, lodging forms and billing chargeable hours, you can see how we began to feel that our worth was judged by the amount of chargeable time that we were able to put out.

This type of framework meant that we were programmed into doing the work ourselves. We were also restricted to generating income during the number of chargeable hours we were able to work in a day, which ultimately restricted the income-earning capacity of the whole business.

By not employing staff to take care of tasks such as invoicing and general administration, our business was getting bogged down.

Consequently, we realised that not only did the business itself have to change, but our attitude towards work had to change too.

We continued to output the work and keep the clients happy, but we also began working **on** the business, as well as **in** the business. This allowed us to make progressive changes to the structure of our business.

We endeavoured to create an environment that was made up of people and systems. Every day, we would come to work asking, "How can this business produce work more efficiently? How can the work get done if we're not here to do it?"

We worked on implementing systems and training people so that they could leverage their time to produce more and to be more efficient. The process involved a significant mindset change over a two-year period, during which time the business went from pending failure to an outstanding success.

## BUSINESS LIFE CYCLE

During this stage of the cycle we discovered that, as business owners, there were five areas that we needed to work on to create growth:

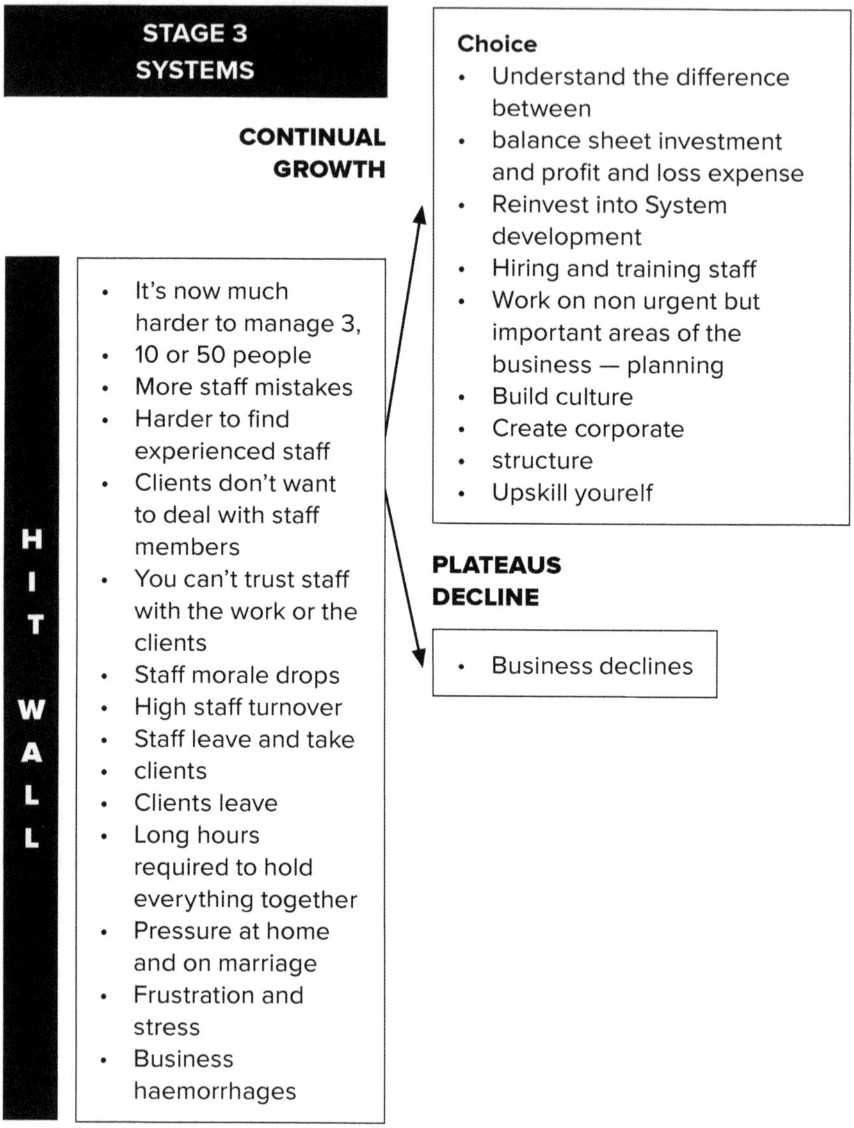

**STAGE 3**
**SYSTEMS**

**HIT WALL**

- It's now much harder to manage 3,
- 10 or 50 people
- More staff mistakes
- Harder to find experienced staff
- Clients don't want to deal with staff members
- You can't trust staff with the work or the clients
- Staff morale drops
- High staff turnover
- Staff leave and take
- clients
- Clients leave
- Long hours required to hold everything together
- Pressure at home and on marriage
- Frustration and stress
- Business haemorrhages

**CONTINUAL GROWTH**

**Choice**

- Understand the difference between
- balance sheet investment and profit and loss expense
- Reinvest into System development
- Hiring and training staff
- Work on non urgent but important areas of the business — planning
- Build culture
- Create corporate
- structure
- Upskill yourelf

**PLATEAUS DECLINE**

- Business declines

### 1. CREATE CAPACITY

Many business owners unknowingly put a lid on the growth of their business simply in the way that they structure their resources, such as their team. Usually, they have their staff and themselves working at 110% capacity.

This results in a scenario whereby you end up turning a lot of business away, because you and your team can't get it done quickly enough. Alternatively, you may unintentionally give the impression that you're too busy to take on any more work.

So the first rule is to ensure your staff members are working at 80–85% capacity, so they can attend to any emergency jobs or work that comes through the door.

### 2. SOW SEEDS

You need to sow seeds constantly so that you can harvest a crop in the future — heaven help the farmer who is so busy harvesting his crop that he forgets to sow seeds in the next field!

Unfortunately, many of us are so busy harvesting that we think we don't need to sow seeds for the future. In actual fact, the opposite is often true.

You need to be in the forefront of your clients' minds when they're ready to do business with you — not just when you're ready to do business with them.

And you can only be at the forefront of their minds if you constantly touch base with them. Research shows that you need to make contact with your clients no less than nine times per year. At a minimum, you shouldn't let three months go by without communicating with them.

We've created a communication system at Chan & Naylor, which involves sending out regular newsletters, emails, Christmas cards and birthday cards, announcing special newsworthy events and presenting regular seminars.

### *3. WORKYOUR CLIENT/CUSTOMER BASE*

Many business owners fail to realise that there is a goldmine of potential new work located within your own database. We're constantly looking for these opportunities to value-add and up-sell to our existing clients and customers, in an effort to attract more business from them and from their network. We can do this because we're not doing the work ourselves. We have others doing the work, which frees up our time to look for these opportunities.

### *3. DIFFERENTIATE YOURSELF*

If you're the same as everybody else and offer the same products and services, you can only be judged by your price. If you offer a unique selling proposition, however, then clients are unable to compare you on price alone — so look for ways to add value to the services you provide.

When we looked at all the successful businesses we knew, we realised that the common theme was that they each specialised in a particular field. Those who specialised became extremely successful, and those who offered generalised services simply survived.

Chan & Naylor's brand didn't really take off until after we had accumulated around 10 years of specialised knowledge in the areas of property investing and structuring, asset protection and estate planning. We then became extremely good at anything to do with property investing, and the word spread: "If you're thinking of investing into real estate, you need to see the people at Chan & Naylor first."

As a result, our reputation was established as the number one accountancy firm in Australia for property investors. To this day, there is very little within the property area for which we cannot find a solution and we've worked hard to build our reputation in this regard.

Even partners from the larger accountancy firms have used our services to set up their own personal affairs in real estate, as we've become known in the marketplace as the number one firm in Australia that specialises in property, and has the expertise and experience in structuring real estate. We also have a branch in nearly every state and territory across the country, and this national presence has helped to attract other national alliances.

Specialisation is so important to your success because in a competitive market, where it's near impossible to stand out amongst the pack, specialisation allows you to differentiate yourself. Also, by being specialists you are honing your skills to be extremely efficient at what you do. This naturally creates efficiencies for your customer or client, resulting in better prices for your clients and better profits for you. It's a win/win for all.

#### *4. INCREASEYOUR BUSINESS*

You can increase your business by 20% without goingoutside your client base, via the following four ways:

a. Increase the number of clients by 5%, by sowing seeds. As mentioned previously, all businesses must constantly keep in touch with their client database. We have had many new clients who have finally come to see us after having attended a seminar or learning about our services seven or eight years earlier. We continually reached out to them with newsletters, emails and regular correspondence and when they were ready to change accountants, we were the obvious choice, as we had been subtly nurturing the relationship over many years.

b. Increase the frequency of transactions by 5%, by increasing your correspondence with existing clients. If a customer is dealing with you once a month, then attempt to offer them a new offering twice a month. This has the amazing result of potentially doubling your turnover. For example, many companies offer sales or one-off promotions that bring the customer backfor a second or third time when they would normally have visited you just once.

c. Increase the average dollar sale by 5%, by packaging and marketing and asking, "Would you like fries with that?" Many businesses do this effectively. McDonalds is the classic example with their pre-packaged meal deals, which encourages customers to upgrade from a single burger purchase. Supermarkets have chocolate bars and magazines at the cashier, in full view of children and paying customers. If executed effectively and consistently, these strategies can be extremely effective. To give you an example of how we did this, we created useful documents and educational DVDs on property investment, structuring, asset protection. The cost of production was minimal we estimated about $3.00 per DVD. These were packaged and given to every client when we delivered the yearly compliance work, not only did this create a point of difference it also created further work and referrals from existing clients. So what can you do in your business to create a point of difference and increase the average dollar sale?

d. Stop the loss of clients by 5%, by implementing loyaltyprograms. Many businesses focus heavily on getting new customers through the door, but they do little to service and retain their existing client base. Studies have shown that it's 60% cheaper to retain your existing customers and sell to them, than it is to try and get new customers, which means that stopping the leakage is a much more cost effective way to increase your profitability.

These concepts and strategies will be addressed in more detail throughout the book.

PART 4

# Planning for Success

There is an old saying: measure twice, cut once. What this actually means in simple terms is that the more time you invest in planning, the fewer problems you're likely to have later on.

Planning is vital if you want to produce a successful outcome. Think of it this way: if you were going to build a house, you wouldn't simply buy a block of land and ask the builder to start laying bricks. You would first engage an architect and sit down to put your vision onto paper to create the house you have dreamed about.

The same applies to your business, so you must start with the end result in mind.

It is simply impossible to work towards a profitable future if you don't know where you're going and, the fact is, the more time you spend on **planning**, the less time you spend on **doing**.

As we were going through the process of creating a business that works — so that we didn't have to — we decided that we needed to sit down and work out exactly what we wanted to achieve. After all, let's face it, how can you possibly know what you want to build if you don't have a vision and plans to build it?

Firstly, we had to work out what we (individually) wanted out of the business. We sat down and wrote a list of the things that we each hoped to personally achieve with the business and we were surprised to discover that our answers were very similar:

1. Generate a passive income stream

2. Restore balance in our lives

3. Choice... the ability to choose whether we work or not, without our income stopping when we stop working

4. To help others through our success

Do you have a roadmap for the future of your business? In his book *The 7 Habits Of Highly Effective People*, Dr Stephen R Covey says that if "you don't plan to fail, you simply fail to plan".

Planning helps us to focus on the 'important, but not urgent' things that we need to attend to in our business. It helps to anticipate and prepare for change. Think of your plan as if it's your blueprint for change in every aspect of your business.

We realised that before we could focus on change in our business, we needed to set our goals and prepare a business plan. One of our goals was to create a business that we, as the owners, did not have to work **in** for 100+ hours each week, as we were doing at the time. So we started delegating work to the team. This gave us more time to work **on** our business.

Next, we identified the key things that we needed to do in order to achieve our goals and this became our business plan, which we like to call our 'action plan'.

This document helped us to stay focused on the critical stages of transformation in our business, and ensured that our key activities were identified and implemented in a logical and practical way.

### ▶ Your business plan will help you do three things:

1. It will clarify your vision and goals regarding what you want your business to look like in the future

2. It will identify where your business is currently placed, and

3. It will determine what work you need to do to close the gap

It is point number three — knowing what work you need to do to close the gap — that forms the basis of your action plan for the year.

It's important to remember that you may come up with hundreds of ideas and strategies regarding things that need to be done, but they can't all be implemented at the same time. In fact, this is one of the reasons why many businesses fail to transform themselves: because there are just too many changes to make and business owners become overwhelmed and do nothing — or they try to do everything at once.

## WORKING SMARTER, NOT HARDER

Change is hard work but it doesn't mean you have to work **harder** in order to achieve results — you just need to work **smarter**.

Making changes and planning for change isn't about spending more hours in the office; it's about focusing your energy on the right tasks. Start by carefully assessing each change based on your 'important, but not urgent' checklist.

Some activities won't be important right now, but they may become important in year two or three of your transformation. Some of our most important activities — for example, 'creating a marketing plan' — didn't occur until the end of the plan. This is because marketing, although vital to future success, wasn't as important during our earlier stages when there were other things that required more urgent attention.

In other words, planning for change will help you set out the priorities of your transformation, ensuring that you focus on the most important changes first.

Once you decide what is most important, you will have the opportunity to work out which resources and skills you need to get the job done. Then you can get started on transforming your business into the thriving empire that you have always dreamed about!

Looking back, we can see that without a doubt, creating a structured business plan was the key ingredient that transformed our business. Think of the last time you tried to make a change in your business without a plan. Was it successful? We remember how hard we worked trying to change our business without putting any planning into it. We got nowhere, until we sat down and worked out where we were, where we wanted to be and what we needed to do to get there.

Once our plan was in place, it kept us on track. We transformed our business entirely and now Chan & Naylor is among the top 20% best performing businesses in the industry!

We recommend that you begin your planning process today. Start by setting your goals so you know exactly what you want your business to look like. You can document your goals using our business plan template and procedure as a starting point.

The Chan & Naylor Strategic Action Plan template was the first plan we ever created, and to this day we still revisit the business plan annually so that we can realign our focus. It has evolved and become more detailed and complex over the years, but we feel that our initial business planning document offers you a great opportunity to make a start.

## CREATING YOUR OWN BUSINESS PLAN

As discussed, the business planning process is a very important step, as it marks the starting point of transforming your business into a money making machine. You should never underestimate the power of putting pen to paper and its ability to help you focus on your goals.

We found that our business plan changed as we moved through different business life cycles, and we quickly recognised that in order to be successful, we would need to treat it as an evolving document. This is vital if you want your business to grow and prosper.

Once we had recognised the importance of the blueprint, we realised that we also required external help in order to properly develop this roadmap. We viewed this as an investment in our Balance Sheet and we sought professional help.

It took several weeks to construct our initial action plan, including a full day spent with a facilitator to create the first draft. As a guide, we worked through the following process:

1. Determined and documented our purpose, mission and core values.

2. Determined what we wanted to achieve with this business, starting with the end goal in mind. In our case, it was life balance, choice and sufficient passive income to maintain our lifestyle.

3. Determined what we wanted the business to look like and formulated goals to reach this vision. For example, what turnover and profit did we need to reach and within what timeframe? What services did we want to offer? How many staff did we need to achieve this?

4. Worked through the numbers. We developed budgets and outlined the turnover and profits we wanted to achieve, based on our business goals and the additional expenses associated with increased staff levels, etc. We worked on a five-year forecast, but it might be more appropriate for you to develop a two, three or 10-year forecast.

5. Brainstormed and prioritised the strategic objectives required to achieve our new goals. Basically, this step was about figuring out what we needed to do to put our plans into action. When you go through this process you may find that there are hundreds of things to do, and this can become daunting once you see the list,but we discovered a strategy to lighten the load.We worked through a matrix to determine which items had the most immediate impact on our business, with the minimal cost and effort involved. These were the 'important, but not urgent' tasks. We narrowed this down to the top five priorities in each area of our business.

6. Determined our point of difference. Assessing where we stood in the marketplace was very important, as we don't just do tax returns, we are property experts and offer strategies to create wealth, protect assets and guide our clients through a myriad of complex tax and financial planning tasks. We needed to know who our competitors were and what our point of difference was, and by taking stock of our product and service offerings, we were able to work out who our ideal client was, which is how we determined that the pharmacy/ nursing type of client was our ideal client (more on this in the next chapter). Just as

importantly, we identified exactly which clients were consuming 80% of our resources and time, but were only generating 20% of our income — and this allowed us to assess the viability of continuing to work with these clients.

7. Completed a SWOT analysis. We set about looking at the **S**trengths and **W**eaknesses of our business and the **O**pportunities and **T**hreats, commonly known as a SWOT analysis. This is like a risk analysis of your business, and it will highlight the different influences — both internally and externally — that may assist or hinder your ability to get this thing done.

8. Reviewed both our and our clients' key frustrations. This may take some time. Often the best way to tap into your clients' frustrations is to simply ask them for feedback. Once you understand any negatives from their point of view, you can go about improving and resolving their frustrations to ensure that their experiences when dealing with your business are always positive. It's important to note that your existing client base provides your best referral source, because they will tell friends and colleagues if they're happy with your service — but if they've had a bad experience, they will tell twice as many people.

9. Developed an action plan. Finally, at this point, we looked at each area of our business and listed tasks or functions that required our attention. Using the same matrix as we did in point 5 above, we prioritised the top five activities in each division. We established an action plan to get these tasks completed, including allocating each task to a person and setting deadlines, so that there was accountability attached to the project.

**PART 5**

# The Four key Drivers of Your Business

As our business developed and grew, and we began to face new challenges, it became clear that we needed help.

In order to make serious headway and transform our fledgling business into a successful, profitable enterprise, we realised that we had to learn the precise drivers of a successful business. It took some time and research but we eventually worked out that the four key drivers listed below are behind every profitable business — regardless of the industry.

| | |
|---|---|
| **Driver 1** | The concept of Grinders, Minders and Finders |
| **Driver 2** | Understand your market and clients |
| **Driver 3** | Ensure you have the right team |
| **Driver 4** | The flow of production within your business |

## DRIVER 1: THE CONCEPT OF GRINDERS, MINDERS AND FINDERS

The first key driver of any business is the owner. It's up to the owner to change the way they see the business and focus on the right type of work, and to do so, they need to understand the concept of Grinders, Minders and Finders. The table below helps to illustrate this concept:

| Doing the work yourself (Working in the factory) | Business works without you | Passive investments |
|---|---|---|
| **WORKING — IN** | **WORKING — ON** | **WORKING — OUT** |
| **Grinding** | **Minding** | **Finding** |
| Short term profits **(Profit & Loss)** | Medium term profits **(Balance Sheet/ ASSET)** | Long term profits **(Balance Sheet/ EQUITY)** |
| • Work in<br>• Work done<br>• Work out<br>• Money collected | • Business model<br>• Culture<br>• Staff training/ Education<br>• Client training/ Education<br>• Upskill Management<br>• Systems | • Passive income generated<br>• Capital Growth<br>• Other Investments<br>• Dividends from Business<br>• Time to work on other opportunities<br>• Other Businesses<br>• Business development<br>• Choice<br>• Build business for sale |

A business owner should strive to spend their time as a Minder and a Finder, rather than a Grinder — but, all too often, this is where the business owner toils.

It's important as a business owner that you hire staff to take care of the grinding work, so that you can spend more time and energy on the other two areas. Owners need to become leaders; you need to get out of the factory and into management. This may mean that you have to find the courage to change the business model, so that the owner isn't also the worker.

## DRIVER 2: UNDERSTAND YOUR MARKET AND CLIENTS

The second key driver of any business is the clients/customers. You must understand what market you're in and who your ideal clients are in order to successfully deliver the right products and services to meet their needs. We defined four broad client types as follows:

### *1. SUPERMARKET CLIENT*

These clients know exactly what they want and, generally, where to get it. They are price sensitive and don't necessarily want extra frills and services. As a simple example, if they have a headache, they decide they need Panadol, walk straight to the medicinal aisle in a supermarket and purchase the cheapest brand on the shelf. If they need chlorine for their pool, they don't seek expert advice or recommendations — they just want to buy the chlorine as cheaply and quickly as possible. Brand loyalty is usually not as important as finding the right product for the best possible price.

### *2. PHARMACY CLIENT*

These clients require a little more assistance and are not as price sensitive as Supermarket clients. For example, if they have a headache, but they want a little bit more assurance and information, they may walk into a pharmacy and ask for advice. Following this, they may still opt to purchase plain old Panadol; however, they're prepared to pay a little extra for the peace of mind and extra service they've received. As another example, a pool owner might drop into a pool shop. Ultimately, the pool owner knows that he needs chlorine, but he might also want his pool water tested. Even though he knows he'll pay a little more for the chlorine at the pool shop rather than a supermarket, he is happy to pay this premium to access the extra service.

### *3. NURSING CLIENT*

These clients require more hands-on assistance and are prepared to pay for it. They know they're sick and they want somebody to nurse them back to health by holding their hand through the process. In general, price isn't a problem as long as they feel they're receiving good service in return. For instance, the pool owner might get someone to come out to his home to clean his pool, test the water and keep the whole system running smoothly.

#### *4. BRAIN SURGERY/SPECIALIST CLIENT*

These clients may know they have a serious problem, but they don't want to know any more details. They just want it fixed and they know it will cost an arm and a leg to do so, but they're prepared to incur that cost. These clients are prepared to pay exorbitant, fees simply so they can get the problem fixed and move on with their lives.

These are very simplistic examples, but they demonstrate how important it is for you as a business owner to understand what market you're in and who your ideal clients are.

Can you guess which client in the above example is the most profitable to your business?

The first option, the Supermarket client, can be very profitable, but you need to be aware that in order to make money, your business needs to be highly efficient and systemised.

In this business, the clients are extremely price sensitive and as a result, running this type of business will generate very low profit margins. The environment is usually very competitive, so high volume is important. There are many examples of successful businesses that target these types of clients and if you can get it right, you may hit the jackpot — just keep in mind that any inefficiency translates to the bottom line very quickly.

The fourth option, the Brain Surgery/Specialist client, is a business that can also be very successful. After all, it's true that specialists such as brain surgeons earn a lot of money.

In such a specialised field, however, it can be more difficult to leverage your efforts. You are the one who earns the money because you're the only one who can do the work.

The problem with this business model is that, although it's wonderful for one's ego to be the only one capable of doing the work, your earning capacity is limited to the number of hours in a day — and when you stop working, you cease producing income. You also burn out very early, which is less than desirable when your income depends on you getting up in the morning and going to work.

For these reasons, (although there are always exceptions to the rule), we have found that the most profitable clients — and therefore the most profitable small business models — are those that are structured around client two and three: the Pharmacy client and the Nursing client.

This is because these clients provide you with the ability to leverage your efforts. In other words, you can get someone else to deliver that service and make a profit margin, without having to do the work yourself. The business doesn't rely on you and when you stop working for whatever reason, such as taking annual leave, your income doesn't cease. Best of all, you won't burn out like many business owners do.

For example, the owner of a pharmacy might pay an employee to carry out the work and they can simply take a profit. He/she doesn't need to attend the premises personally and if he/she owned several other pharmacies, then they would earn more money. He/she is also able to take annual leave without worrying that his income will cease.

If you had a Nursing type of a business, such as a home cleaning pool service, then you could also pay an employee to carry out the work while you simply take a profit from the business.

In both of these areas, the ability to leverage is vital, as the business doesn't just rely on one person, product or idea.

You may own a business that currently qualifies as catering to Brain Surgery clients, but you can turn it into a Nursing business. Perhaps you own a business that sells specialist water filters. If so, you could add a Nursing element by providing a service for the repair, installation and/or cleaning of these specialist filtering systems.

Car magnate Henry Ford is perhaps the most famous example of business smarts when it comes to understanding this concept of Brain Surgery versus Nursing business. He once famously said that he would give away all of his cars for free, as long as he maintained the spare parts division.

At Chan & Naylor, we recognised that there was a market for the Pharmacy and Nursing type of client within the financial services industry. Research showed us that clients wanted hand holding and specialist advice in complex areas of running their business, such as asset protection, structuring of property investments, estate planning, tax minimisation, wealth creation and self-managed superannuation funds.

Therefore, we were able to create a 'one-stop shop' for clients so they could access every service they required, across generations.

## DRIVER 3: ENSURE YOU HAVE THE RIGHT TEAM

The third key driver of your business is your team. The only way you'll be able to effectively run and grow a business is by leveraging through your staff.

It's all very well to say that you make money by leveraging through the use of your people, but those of us who have lost a lot of money trying to leverage into small business, property or the share market know only too well that leveraging comes with risks.

Leveraging magnifies the situation, which means that it transforms good things into great things — but the flipside of that coin is that if you leverage a bad situation, you may magnify your problems.

Therefore, if you don't know how to manage your team to get the best from them, you could create huge problems for yourself, which could result in huge losses.

We realised early on that it's very difficult to manage people and, as a result, we needed to create and implement the right systems to help us manage our staff.

We also learnt that clients have different expectations of what service means to them. Good service to one client means calling them every week to provide ongoing support, while good service to another client is a phone call to check in twice a year. We knew that we had to bring individual clients' expectations up or down to match our standard, so we set about managing our clients' expectations,

which in turn helped us to manage the staff. The system we adopted is EMRR (pronounced 'Emma').

**E:** From the very beginning, establish **EXPECTATIONS** for your team and your clients. We use various systems such as budgets for team members, which help set standards, goals and work culture. For clients, we use correspondence, newsletters and price lists to help establish expectations.

**m: mONITOR** and **mANAGE** your team so they can reach their targets, but never do the work **for** them. Regularly communicate with your clients and your team to keep them informed of any changes within the business.

**R:** You must measure the **RESUlTS** of everything you do, because what you can measure, you can manage. Our team performance is measured by feedback from regular client surveys, and we measure our staff members' fee budgets monthly. Consequently, each team member's results are measured by the quality of the surveys received from their clients and their financial/budget performance.

**R:** We **REWARD** our staff on a regular basis with bonus systems and a Star Award system, which we'll talk about in more detail in a later chapter. We are big believers in rewarding people on a regular basis, so rather than waiting until the end of the year to give them a bonus, we offer smaller, more regular rewards such as social staff outings and lunches to celebrate achieving milestones.

### *GET IT RIGHT UPFRONT*

Getting the right team in place is a critical driver for the growth and success of your business. Your team is the pathway to success and while many business owners view this as a cost (Profit & Loss) to their business, in real terms, if managed correctly, your people are an investment in the organisation (Balance Sheet).

The only time your people become a cost is when you hire incorrectly and you don't have the systems and training in place to correct the problem. This is why we have applied the "hire slow, fire fast" principle, because if you're in a rush to fill a vacancy, you'll be less likely to appoint the right person for the job. And, at the end of the day, it's all about getting the right person in the right seat on the right bus.

At Chan & Naylor we invest a lot of time and money into recruitment because we understand how costly it can be to get this wrong. We now have a human resources department, which manages the flow of staff, but no matter how big or small your business, the same principles apply.

In the early days we didn't have the capacity or resources to pay recruitment agencies or invest in expensive personality profiling, so we developed a basic system for evaluating new staff members.

We had a standard checklist of questions to ask each potential employee, which was designed to bring out their personality.

We also had a questionnaire that asked the applicant various technical questions, the purpose of which was to give us an accurate indication of their skill-set to get the job done.

Along the way, we also up-skilled ourselves and attended various human resource seminars, so that we could understand some of the science behind the human condition. From this, we developed a basic personality test to determine whether each applicant was right for that particular role.

This was a very inexpensive and perhaps a primitive form of profiling, but we found that the results were uncannily accurate and this system was successful.

We based our profiling on four personality types:

1. The 'get things done' personality (Focuser)

2. The 'get along' personality (Relater)

3. The 'get appreciated' personality (Integrator)

4. The 'get it right' personality (Operator)

We understood the types of personalities that suited particular roles within the industry. For example, our client managers and customer service staff had to have the type of personality where they would 'get along' with a wide range of people and 'get things done', as they were dealing with clients face to face and needed to build strong relationships.

However, if we were hiring a bookkeeper or somebody for a support role where no client/customer contact was required, we would need a staff member who could 'get things done' and 'get it right'.

Alternatively, if we were hiring a receptionist, we required someone with a 'get along' type of personality.

Ed, for example, is a 'get things done' and 'get it right' personality, whereas David is a 'get things done' and 'get along' person. We both understand this, so when David undertakes a task and gets it done, and presents it to Ed for review, he knows that Ed will ensure the detail is correct as he aims to 'get it right'. This is a priority for Ed **before** he gets it done — and this is one reason why we work so well together, because we understand our respective strengths and weaknesses, and we allocate responsibilities accordingly.

In fact, it is essential that you understand various personalities and the strengths and weaknesses of the people you work with. The business owners and directors on a Board should understand each other, just as the staff of any organisation should understand each other, as this can facilitate the allocation of appropriate functions and alleviate frustrations amongst your team.

Think about it this way: if you know that Jane is a 'get it right' personality, then you know that she will do an excellent job with tasks that require great attention to detail.

If you need the job turned around very quickly, however, Jane might not be the right person to turn to, as she prioritises 'getting it right' over 'getting it done'.

Think of how many conflicts could be avoided within any business if we simply had a better understanding of how our fellow workers operated!

To implement this at Chan & Naylor, we held staff training sessions with our employees to help them understand each other. In a group session, we asked each staff member to complete the personality profile. We then asked another staff member to review this and discuss their personality profile. The results were amazingly accurate, and helped everyone to appreciate their co-workers' personalities, strengths and weaknesses.

With this system in place, we started to hire more staff and were able to place them in the right seat on the right bus. As a result, we experienced lower staff turnover.

These days, we have a much more complicated profiling system with more complex outcomes (there are many organisations that outsource this function), but the principles are still the same as our original evaluation questionnaires.

Just a note: we always undertake reference checks with previous employers, as past performance is always a good indicator of future performance.

### *REGULAR FEEDBACK TO YOUR TEAM*

Many business owners fail to realise that hiring a team member is only part of the human resource process. It is such a pity that so many managers and team leaders consider performance reviews to be a waste of time, because they really are so valuable. When correctly designed and implemented, regular performance reviews can be a crucial tool in helping to develop and grow your people and your business.

Each of your team members will benefit from any coaching, mentoring, guidance and constructive feedback you provide. As you can imagine, this level of maintenance involves a decent amount of time and commitment from both you and them, in order to function productively.

Let's get all the negatives out of the way first. Yes, performance reviews take time — time to prepare, time to conduct and time to follow up. They can be tiring and draining, especially when staff members are reluctant to get involved. And, of course, the time that you and your team members spend on performance reviews is time away from doing client work.

However, if you only focus on the negatives, then performance reviews will always be considered an inconvenience. Conducting meaningful performance reviews starts with the right attitude, because if you're not on board, then how can you expect your staff to contribute value to the process?

We learnt to look at performance reviews not as a cost of our time (Profit & Loss), but as an investment of our time into our Assets (Balance Sheet). When viewed in this light, it's clear that regular reviews are essential to the success of our team and our business.

Having the right attitude plays a big role in the process of performance reviews because it will guide how well you prepare for them, conduct them and how you communicate their importance to your team members.

A meaningful performance review looks at three key areas:

- **Past performance**: How did the staff member perform during the review period?

- **Current development needs**: What skills and experience does the staff member need to continue to perform at the expected level?

- **Future goals**: Next year's performance goals and personal career objectives.

The work that you have done throughout the year in coaching each team member and raising issues and concerns as soon as they arise should mean that your discussion of past performance is going to be relatively short. You might only spend 15 minutes going over what happened during the year. With that out of the way, you then have plenty of time to discuss the future with your team member.

Conducting meaningful performance reviews therefore becomes a matter of GAPPS:

- Gathering facts and figures: These support your assessment of your team member's performance.

- Attitude of participants: Think of the review process as a formal conclusion to the year and an important part of business growth.

- Preparation, preparation, preparation: This is key. Boring and useless reviews are the result of poor planning and preparation.

- Planning for reactions: Put yourself in your team member's shoes to gauge how they might react.

- Skills and development needs: What skills, education, knowledge or experience does the team member need to move to the next level?

During your career you may have had reviews that were a waste of time. Think back to why that was. In most cases, either the reviewer or the participant may have been unprepared, or the review was rushed, or perhaps the discussion was one-sided. In all of these scenarios, what transpired was not a genuine review process where open and honest conversation was encouraged. If this has been your experience, now is the time to change it!

Performance reviews should be a valuable exercise for both the manager and the staff member. To help you conduct the most effective and meaningful performance reviews possible, we've outlined some tips and guidelines below.

- **There should be no surprises.** A performance review should be a summary of the discussions that have taken place during the year. If you're bringing up poor performanceissuesthatrelatetosomethingthathappened months ago, you're not using the right approach. If your staff member did something wrong days, weeks or months ago, by waiting to bring it up in the review, you're sending the message that performance reviews are an opportunity to have a go at your staff members.

- Instead, discuss poor performance when it occurs and, if necessary address it once more in the review. Ensure that you set clear goals and do not move the posts unless you have both agreed to re-set expectations — because by constantly changing the goalposts, you risk demoralising and demotivating the team.

- **Play the ball, not the man.** This means as a manager of people, you should focus on correcting the activity rather than criticising the person. For example, this means saying, "John, a better result may have been achieved if it was handled this way," vs. "John, you did it the wrong way". You should also avoid the use of the word **'you'** as this can be taken as a personal attack. It's much better to say, "A few mistakes have been made John," rather than "John you have made a few mistakes".

- **Take your time — don't rush**. Rushing reviews gives the impression that you don't view the team member as being important. Take as much time as you need and avoid doing more than three reviews per day, as they can be very tiring.

- **Avoid interruptions**. Don't answer the phone and don't allow other staff members to interrupt you during a review. Ignoring all other distractions confirms to your team member that they are the most important person to you at this time and it also provides a great opportunity to reinforce the importance of the review.

- **Talk less and listen more**. A meaningful performance review is one where the staff member is doing most of the talking. You should be guiding the discussion and putting your views forward when necessary, but in general the staff member should be discussing their performance.

- **The same applies to discussions about skill development**. This is a great opportunity to reinforce the responsibility that your staff members have in paving their own future. Encourage them to discuss where they need to improve, what new skills and experience they need to develop, and how they are going to achieve them.

- **Relax**. Some managers tend to adopt a whole new persona when conducting performance reviews. Reviews are far more meaningful when you are yourself and talk to your team members as you would on any other day. Becoming stiff and formal during a review is going to make your staff member nervous and take some of the focus off the purpose of the meeting.

- **Be prepared.** This applies to both the manager and the staff member. Some managers refuse toconducta review when a staff member hasn't prepared, because reviews are only meaningful when both parties have invested time and thought into the process. Encouraging staff members to prepare for their review reinforces the need for them to take responsibility for their development and be accountable for their performance.

- **Finally, follow up**. All of your hard work will be for nothing if, after the review, none of the agreed actions or development needs is put into effect. Schedule follow- up sessions to book training, review work or brief other staff members who will be coaching staff. Make diary notes to follow up staff members who have agreed to look into training or seek the help of a colleague.

### *MOTIVATING YOUR TEAM*

Many people think that motivating your team requires simply doing those little extras, like taking them to lunch or arranging team-bonding sessions. Although these ideas are great and do assist, they are only temporary fixes and generally the motivation only lasts a few days.

Instead, we have found that if you combine productivity with the above activities, then maintaining motivation is much more sustainable. When people are productive, and they achieve their workload — whether it involves completing projects, finishing tasks or achieving sales — morale lifts.

It's amazing how people's energy and attitudes change, and the impact that it can have on the organisation as a whole, when productivity and morale is high. If you are having issues with your team's morale, consider organising certain projects and tasks for people to do, with a focus on completing the task and having achievable measurable outcomes.

Achieving a result and completing a project, either individually or as a team, is amazingly effective at increasing the spirits of everyone in your organisation, and can be much more sustainable then a "quick fix" morale booster.

## DRIVER 4: THE FLOW OF PRODUCTION WITHIN YOUR BUSINESS

The fourth key driver in any business is workflow and production, which is basically how things move through the organisation to result in a product or service delivered to the market.

This refers to internal processes such as how to get the work in and the product produced, and how to get the work out, the invoices raised and the cash collected — as a sale is not a sale until the money has been banked.

Imagine for a moment that your product or service is a particle. Those particles should flow smoothly through the organisation and come out the other end as a product or service, with the end result being a delighted client.

Unfortunately, what typically tends to happen within a disorganised business is that the particles bounce chaotically around the organisation, which creates inefficiency. The reason for this is that there is inadequate organisational structure, processes or systems in place to facilitate all of the particles flowing in a smooth, orderly fashion throughout the organisation.

An organisational chart represents the flow of work from the moment it comes in the front door to the moment it leaves the organisation. There are basically six divisions in our organisational chart:

### *SECTION 1: BOARD OF DIRECTORS, OR OWNERS*

The Board is usually comprised of people who have all the ideas of what the company should be doing. Their job is to ensure that their ideas and goals are implemented by the team.

### *SECTION 2: PROMOTIONS & MARKETING DIVISION*

The person responsible for this division is responsible for exposing the company to people who have never heard of them. In order to do this, they need to get involved in seminars, organise PR campaigns, send regular communications (such as newsletters) and engage in other marketing strategies to boost the profile of the business.

### *SECTION 3: SALES & CUSTOMER SERVICE DIVISION*

This division is responsible for converting a 'prospect' into a 'customer'. For example, a prospect may show interest in the company's products through the efforts of Section 2. This prospect is then passed to Section 3, where a salesman attempts to sell the company's products or services to convert them into a client/customer.

### *SECTION 4: PRODUCTION & MANUFACTURING DIVISION*

This is where the product or service is actually produced and delivered to the customer.

### *SECTION 5: ACCOUNTS DIVISION*

As the financial hub of any organisation, the accounts division is where the money is collected, bills are paid and statistics are gathered to enable the correct measurement of key performance indicators. What you can measure, you can manage; without proper statistics showing trends and patterns of performance, you are really flying blind.

### *SECTION 6: IMPLEMENTATION DIVISION*

This division brings the managing director's ideas to life. Implementation of ideas is the secret to a successful, profitable business and yet, unfortunately, this division is missing in most organisations. As a result, many great ideas are never implemented because no one is made personally responsible for seeing the idea through. You may have heard the phrase that success is 20% inspiration and 80% perspiration. What this really means is that it's better to have fewer ideas with greater implementation, rather than many great ideas with little implementation.

## ROLES & RESPONSIBILITIES

Your organisational chart will also outline the roles and responsibilities of the people who work within your business.

The managing director is responsible for the delegation of tasks to the rest of the team, and he or she is ultimately responsible for holding each staff member accountable for their tasks.

Too many managing directors are task-oriented rather than management-oriented, meaning they veer towards doing the work themselves rather than effectively delegating it. Often this is because they believe that if they want it done right, they have to do it themselves.

This is the biggest mistake made by most small business owners. Their role is not to do the work themselves, but to train and teach their staff to do the work for them.

Their role is more like a coach in a soccer game. He doesn't launch himself onto the playing field and hold a position during the game. Instead, his role is to motivate, train and inspire his team to get the best results out of the people he has on the field. He needs to get the team working together, as a group in harmony will create tremendous synergy, efficiency and leverage. In the business world, this all translates to profits on the bottom line.

Quite often, the business owner who is evolving from a technician into a manager can't help but jump in and do the work themselves. They may think that they can do the task better or faster, but at the same time they don't realise that they're neglecting their own job, which is to 'manage', not to 'do'.

Eventually, what ends up happening is that the employee feels like they're being undermined. They will generally sit back and let you do the work, as you haven't instilled in them the confidence to give it a go themselves. Ultimately, you'll end up doing all of the work, but with a paid audience — one that you're footing the bill for! The employee also won't take responsibility for the tasks they're meant to be performing, and there is no way of measuring productivity and holding that person accountable for the job, because you've done all the work yourself.

Finally, by following this path you haven't passed your experience down to the next person, which means that everyone will keep coming back to you for advice.

At this stage, some of you might be thinking, "But what if I train them and impart all of the skills and knowledge that I've learnt over the years — and then they up and leave?"

Well, that could very well happen. But what happens if you **don't** train them, and they stay?

It is much better that a position is left empty than a position is filled by an employee who doesn't have the right skills and training for the role.

Training your employees will give you much more than it will take, as it will allow you to leverage your time. Eventually, the trained employee will be able to do the tasks that you used to do, and the more people you have doing tasks and generating income, the more profitable you will become — and the closer you come to building a business that works without you.

Yes, it's true that some people will leave and take their experience with them. For this reason, it's absolutely imperative that you build systems and training manuals that not only allow you to quickly and efficiently train the new recruit, but also retain any intellectual property that has been developed. At the end of the day, the value of your business is not what is between your ears, but rather what is written in the manuals and anchored to the business.

The more your business is systematised and the less it is reliant on your input, the more valuable it is to a prospective buyer. You may not be interested in selling your business, but you should always run your business as though it's for sale, because it means that you're working towards a framework where the business can work without you — and that is what ultimately gives you 'choice' in life.

**PART 6**

# Organising the Business

If there was one area within Chan & Naylor that we knew we could improve upon in those early days, it was the way that we organised our business.

We've come to learn that this is one of the most important aspects of small business ownership, as it creates the structure or framework that the business is based upon.

Small businesses, by definition, generally have a small number of employees. As a result, there's usually not a great deal of formality associated with the business's organisational structure.

This is one of the most common mistakes that small business owners make, particularly when the business is a family-run affair. This lack of formality can unintentionally create a secretive, guarded environment whereby decisions are not properly discussed or communicated with staff, because you may assume they know what is happening and why, or you may feel that they don't need to know. In fact, the opposite is true. When there is no overall organisational structure guiding the development of the business, and your staff members are not involved in the process, they will more than likely have no idea why particular decisions are made — and they certainly won't feel like they're involved in the process.

As a quick example, let's assume that you own a small business with four staff members. One of your employees, Tom, asks for an assistant, as he is struggling with his workload and needs help attending to his administrative tasks. You tell Tom that hiring an assistant isn't financially feasible right now, but you can revisit the idea again next financial year.

Four weeks later, you hire a new staff member — a sales person whose job is to generate more income for the business. You've been planning to add this person to the team for some time, and with the extra revenue they bring in, you will be able to hire at least a part- time support staff member to help take the administrative load off all of your employees.

However, Tom doesn't know this. When Tom asked about hiring an assistant, all he heard in response was: "There's not enough money in the kitty to hire a new staff member right now." Yet, just weeks later, a new sales person has joined the team… and Tom is not happy. After all, as far as Tom is aware, "There's not enough money in the kitty to hire a new staff member right now."

If Tom — and in fact, all of your staff members — had been across your organisational structure, and had been aware of your plans and goals for the business, they would understand why you hired a new sales person. More importantly, they would have felt valued in the decision-making process and therefore, able to take ownership of the result.

This is just a basic example, but it demonstrates how vital communication and organisation is within your business, regardless of how big or small.

After reading *The E Myth,* we realised that in order to create a business that works without being dependant on us physically working in it, we had to treat our small business as if it was a large corporation — even though we only had a handful of staff members. This meant that we needed to have clear lines of responsibility, so that each of our employees knew who was responsible for what within the organisation.

## ORGANISATIONAL CHARTS

Every business, no matter how large or small, should have an organisational chart. We touched on the importance and functions of an organisational chart in Chapter 5, but we'll now explore its value in more detail.

As mentioned earlier, we came to think of our business as a big processing plant. Business comes in the door, like disorganised particles bouncing around the walls, and these particles need to be organised so that they flow smoothly through the business. Ultimately, they flow out the other side in the form of a polished service and/or product.

In any small business there is always work to be done, whether it's the 'nuts and bolts' factory floor work of producing products and services, or the back-end strategic tasks of planning, reviewing, organising and managing.

An organisational chart is a way of representing jobs and their functions, the various areas of job responsibility, and reporting relationships. They can help us answer questions such as, what are the tasks that need to be completed? Who is responsible for each task? How are these tasks going to be divided up among staff and, if problems arise, who is the go-to person for answers or guidance?

The best way to create accountability and responsibility is to organise your business around the functions of the business, such as administration, marketing, IT, human resources and sales. Your organisational chart will then need people in charge and accountable for each of these functions.

You can start creating your own organisational chart by asking:

- What jobs or tasks need to be done?
- Which department of the business do these tasks fall under (administration, marketing, etc)?
- How many people are required (full-time, part-time or casual) to get each task done?
- Who is responsible for each department?

This may seem like overkill in the early stages when you only have two or three staff members, but it's important that you set these structures and procedures up from the very beginning, to guide the growth of your business in an organised way.

When we initially drew up an organisational chart and started putting names in the respective boxes, we noticed an interesting pattern. Unsurprisingly, our names appeared at the top of every single box!

We knew that this was not the right solution moving forward, so we divided up the different areas of the business and made each other accountable for various departments. Our organisational chart was a very important document that helped us to realise just how many roles we were undertaking within the business.

### JOB DESCRIPTIONS

Next, we began the process of creating job descriptions so that every staff member knew what was expected of their role.

The aim of a job description is to explain the main duties, responsibilities and tasks of that particular position. We've found that it's best to keep them as simple and concise as possible, so there's less chance of confusion.

Job descriptions are an important tool when hiring new team members and they also help in the training process. As a general guide, they should include:

- The correct position title
- The required qualifications
- The level of responsibility
- Who that person reports to
- Who reports to them
- Their accountabilities or tasks

When we created position descriptions to suit Chan & Naylor in the early days, we agreed to appoint one of us as the general manager. We were starting with our end goal in mind, as we knew that we wanted to replace our names with those of other team members as we grew and developed the appropriate systems and procedures.

As with organisational charts, position descriptions are evolving documents and will need to be reviewed and updated from time to time. Staffing requirements should always be on the agenda of your regular team meetings, as your business's staffing needs will change over time.

As the team leader and employer, it's up to you to make sure that staff levels and skills match the requirements of the business. Are more employees needed in a particular area? Are more employees needed at a particular time of day? Do the roles of existing staff need to be reviewed? As your business evolves, these issues will need to be continually monitored and addressed when necessary.

### *EMPOWERING YOUR STAFF*

Once you have established your organisational chart and written up job descriptions, and you've allocated responsibility to each role within your business, you must train and empower your staff to take on their respective roles.

This is where your inner control freak can come back to haunt you. The old fears that you've held for years may stand in your way, as you worry that the client will leave if you don't handle their work personally, or service levels will drop. If you want to get ahead, however, you must move on from these fears so that your staff members can get on with the job in a controlled, measurable fashion. In the early days, we definitely suffered from the control freak syndrome. The best solution we could come up with to manage this was to establish systems to measure these fears, which resulted in the EMMR described in a previous chapter.

In a professional services industry like accounting, where the business is highly relationship based, it was a big shift to step back, empower our staff members and simply '**let go**'. But, if we did it, then there's no reason why it can't be done in other industries.

Here are some of the systems that we put in place to help us through this transition:

1. We established budgets. Each team member was assigned their own personal budget, which included the names and details of the clients that they were to manage. These were reviewed weekly.

2. We carefully managed the handover process from ourselves to each staff member, and personally introduced the new client manager to the client. We managed our clients' expectations by explaining the benefits of having a team working for them, rather than just one individual.

3. We developed a 'peace of mind' guarantee and evaluation surveys to facilitate regular communication and feedback of performances (we'll talk about this in more detail in a later chapter).

4. We established communication lines with our database so that it was the organisation, and not just an individual, that built relationships with our clients. This was achieved by sending out monthly newsletters and correspondence that managed client expectations, by reinforcing the name of the client manager, so that they became more comfortable turning to that staff member for expert advice.

5. We itemised our services and created price lists, so our staff could talk about fees and services directly with the client.

6. We trained our staff on soft skills and active listening skills, which gave them the armoury to deal with client complaints and issues. This not only gave our employees an added skill-set, but it also took this responsibility away from us.

## THE DANGER OF BYPASSING

Once you have empowered your staff and created clear lines of communication through job descriptions and your organisational chart, your next step is to put systems in place to manage everything effectively.

It's important that you communicate how each system and process works to every member of your team, so that you can free yourself of the day-to-day issues that bog you down. There's no point going to the effort of establishing all of the above, only to have it all come crashing down if nothing is implemented properly.

In the early days of implementation, you may come across scenarios where either the client or a staff member will 'bypass' the person responsible for that particular situation, and they'll go straight up the chain of command to bring the issue directly to you. If you encourage this type of behaviour or you don't immediately correct this flow, you'll be doomed to fail, as you'll be right back where you started — with an overflowing inbox and a to- do list as long as your arm. You need to stop, reinforce and educate the people involved about the correct flow, and redirect them to the appropriate person.

If you let it slide "just this once" and allow bypassing to happen, two things will occur:

1. You will take on the work that you're trying to delegate, which defeats the purpose.

2. You will undermine the person in charge of that area, which creates a whole new set of relationship issues.

For example, let's say that you have appointed a staff member, Emily, to manage a portfolio of clients. Emily is also responsible for managing three sales people who report directly to her on all matters. One of her sales people, Paul, has been assisting Emily with a particularly large client and discusses new pricing on the products.

Paul negotiates a price with the client and goes directly to you, the owner, to seek approval. In other words, Paul has bypassed Emily.

If you agree without involving Emily, you will have bypassed her and undermined her position. A better solution would be to redirect Paul to discuss the situation directly with Emily, or you could meet with both Emily and Paul at the same time to discuss the situation as a team.

Bypassing can occur up, down and across the chain of command, and it can be frustrating and demoralising to all parties involved. Therefore, when a situation such as this occurs you must ensure that all of your staff members understand who they report to, and exactly who is responsible for which areas of the business.

To take this concept a step further, we have our organisational chart on display within our office so that everyone is aware of their own responsibilities, and their fellow team members' responsibilities. We have also trained them on the principles of bypassing.

There is only one acceptable instance when bypassing should be permitted, and that is when a situation places your business in a precarious position, and it is imperative that action is taken immediately.

In our previous example using Emily and Paul, let's assume that Paul has been negotiating with the client and has had several discussions with Emily about the proposed pricing structure. After many meetings and conversations, Emily has not acted, and the client has complained to Paul about the lack of activity. The client has even threatened to take his business elsewhere, and yet, Emily still hasn't acted on the matter.

In this instance, it would be acceptable for Paul to bypass Emily and go directly to you as the business owner to inform you of the situation. It would then be up to you to: a) make a decision regarding the client; and b) investigate why Emily isn't working in an efficient and effective manner.

This type of situation is an emergency and it's important to remember that once the emergency has been handled, the task must be handed back to the person who was originally responsible for it. After all, the ultimate goal is to stop the flow of work hitting your desk so that you can concentrate all of your energy on working **on** the business — not **in** it.

### *MEETING YOUR CLIENTS' NEEDS*

Many years ago we introduced a guarantee on our services to back up our customer service commitment. We were one of the first accounting firms in Australia to adopt this form of guarantee and once again, the industry said it couldn't be done.

However, we found that our guarantee generated a great deal of trust between the firm and our clients, which served as a brilliant opportunity to build our relationships and ensure that we were meeting the needs of our clients. The guarantee was issued with every service we provided and it was a great tool to build trust and also manage our clients' expectations.

It also became and effective tool to manage the team indirectly, because the guarantee was signed by the partner and also the team member completing the service. Therefore, the team member was signing off that all components of the service were being completed to a high standard.

Our guarantee and subsequent surveys were introduced and implemented for five reasons. Firstly, they offer a quality point of difference that separates Chan & Naylor from our competitors. It comes back to that golden rule: if you are different from everybody else, you cannot be judged on price alone.

Secondly, they provided and effective way to managing our team. Remember it is difficult to manage people without systems, so don't try — instead, create systems to manage people. Our guarantee sets out nine standard points of expectations on behalf of the client. Every time a team member signs a guarantee, it reinforces in their mind what is expected of them. This works better than having a manager standing over them, constantly on their back.

In the course of a flight, an aircraft will usually veer off-course for around 90% of the journey, and it is the pilot's job to constantly correct the plane and keep it heading the right direction. People sometimes forget to do things in the course of their work, just as a plane will naturally go off course — so it is systems like this that will keep them on track.

The survey that is completed by the client serves to give us valuable feedback and is used as a system to manage staff. If the team member is aware that they are being rated on every aspect of their client contact, they become more motivated to meet the standards expected of them.

The third reason we introduced surveys and guarantees is to educate the clients as to the training we go through, and the "five minute type" free phone calls that our firm offers. Indirectly, this lets them know that impromptu conversations lasting more than five minutes will be billed.

The fourth reason is marketing. We are able to use the surveys to contact clients about other services that we offer such as loans, financial planning and insurance.

Finally, our surveys provide the client with a welcome opportunity to comment on our service and make suggestions on how we can improve further. Every business can benefit from this type of feedback.

## PART 7

# Systems, Systems, Systems

Systems are vital to the success of your business, as they will enable you to leverage your time more productively.

No matter what industry you're in, as the owner of the business your aim should be to ensure that your team delivers a consistent, high quality product or service to your client or customer, without you having to do the work.

The right systems, when they're simple to implement and consistently used, make this possible, as systems take the discretion away from the operational level. They also improve the efficiency and consistency of workflow through your operation, and allow you to work **on** your business, rather than **in** your business. Even more importantly, they serve to increase the overall **value** of your business. Once we had designed our business plan and prepared our organisational chart, which set out who was responsible for what, we began to work on implementing the changes. The big question

was, how?

We were already working 80 to 100 hours per week, and our families, health and wellbeing were being neglected. How could we squeeze more hours into a week to work **on** the business, when we already had our hands full working **in** the business?

We realised through re-education that it's not about 'doing'

it's about 'managing'. It's not about doing one thing 100 times better; it's about doing 100 things 1% better.

In other words, there were small changes and tweaks that we could make to improve our working life and our business. At the end of the day, it's not the product or the type of service that you provide that makes the difference between a successful and an unsuccessful business — it's how you deliver that product or service.

For instance, there might be two courier companies operating in the exact same market, offering the exact same service (delivering parcels), yet one courier company may be much more successful than the other. The difference is simply how the business is managed. When one courier company does 100 things 1% better than the other, they subsequently achieve better results.

It all comes down to the way the business is managed. By ensuring that the little things in your business are looked after, you can be assured that the big picture will look after itself.

As the manager and leader in your business, your role should cover three areas:

1. Systems, systems, systems: developing and improving them.

2. Recruiting: surrounding yourself with the best people.

3. Training, training, training: coach both your staff and your clients to do things the way you want them done. Rather than doing the work for them, show them by teaching, supporting and nurturing them to produce the best they can possibly produce.

At this point it's important to reinforce that in order to be an effective manager, you may need to change the way you look at your employees. Rather than being something that costs you money — a Profit & Loss cost — you need to view staff salaries as an expense that helps you to make money — a Balance Sheet investment.

Instead of thinking, "The more staff I have, the more it's costing me," try changing your thinking to, "The more staff I have, the more money I'm making." Provided that you recruit and manage them appropriately, this will be precisely the case.

By adopting this mindset, you can then begin to leverage your efforts through your staff and systems.

Think of it this way. Imagine you have 10 staff who are each looking after 150 clients, and you help them to each produce **net** profits (after their own wages and overheads) of $50,000 annually, for a total profit of $500,000. Wouldn't it be much easier to manage these staff to help them reach their goals rather than look after 1,500 clients to generate that income yourself?

In his book *The E-Myth,* Michael Gerber explains that most businesses are comprised of four key areas:

1. Marketing

2. Administration

3. Operations

4. Human Resources

Most business owners spend all of their time in Operations, where they produce the product or service, and very little time in the other areas. This is akin to a car that's only got one of its cylinders working; the car would run very roughly, and certainly not efficiently.

As the owner of the business, you must ensure that sufficient time and effort is dedicated to each of the areas of your business. The only way that there can be sufficient time for this to occur, is if you hire and train employees to produce the Operations work on your behalf.

This will then free up your time so you can do the right kind of work: that is, **managing** and not **doing**.

## THE BENEFITS OF SYSTEMS

Involving your team in the development and implementation of a system will allow them to take ownership, which is extremely important for a system's ultimate success.

There are several ways in which systems will make your business run more smoothly, such as:

- They provide consistency and uniformity in the delivery of your services and/or products.

- They provide a structured working environment for your team.

- They provide a quick and efficient training process for your team.

- They leverage staff with the lowest skill level to perform high-level tasks.

- They make team members accountable, as there are clear lines of responsibility.

- They offer the business owner more time and therefore a better lifestyle.

- They provide choice to the business owner as the business continues to work, even if the owner does not.

- They ultimately increase the saleable value of the business.

You may wonder why it is that some people can maintain great levels of sales success while others cannot. Ask any good sales person and, chances are, they'll tell you they have a system in place for selling. It might relate to the questions they ask, the answers they have, the strategies they employ for building customer relationships, or the tools and techniques they use to add value and build trust with customers.

You see, great sales-people have worked out, through trial and error, what works for them, and they know that by duplicating their most successful strategies, they can maximise the chance of a successful outcome again.

You may have experienced this yourself. A customer contacts your business, you say all of the right things and, bingo, you've made a sale. Ten minutes later another customer comes in, you say something different and that customer walks away without having bought anything.

If only you had duplicated what it was that you said the first time. Well, with a system in place, this is exactly what you can achieve — and it works for more than just sales.

Everything you do in your business should be systemised to get the best possible result every time.

McDonald's, the international fast food juggernaut, has got it right. They have a system in place for everything they do, from ordering stock, to cooking the burger patties, to serving the customers. Everyone knows the "Do you want fries with that?" routine. Why do they do it? Because it maximises the results they achieve.

Your business may not be McDonald's, but regardless of your company's size or the industry you are in, systems are just as important, because they will ensure that you maximise your chances of achieving the best results — not only in sales, but also in areas like error reduction, time savings, customer service and efficiency.

Let's look at some of the things that should be systemised in your own business to help you get better results. Some of these may seem more or less important than others, but you should consider developing systems in all of the following areas of your business:

- ✔ Sales
- ✔ Customer service
- ✔ The correspondence you send to your customers/ clients
- ✔ How the customer is treated on the telephone
- ✔ How the customer is received in your store
- ✔ The timing of your deliveries
- ✔ The time it takes to return calls
- ✔ Your promptness in keeping appointments
- ✔ The presentation of your products

- ✔ The level of your after-sales service
- ✔ The way you handle complaints
- ✔ Job descriptions
- ✔ Role definitions
- ✔ The tasks your staff perform
- ✔ The goals your staff are expected to achieve
- ✔ The parameters your staff have to work within
- ✔ Staff members' understanding of who to report to
- ✔ Ongoing training

This may seem like system overkill, but we can assure you, once you have invested your time, money and energy into setting up the correct systems, your business will run like a well-oiled machine. If you're feeling a little overwhelmed by the tasks ahead, consider starting with the follow key areas:

## STRATEGIC SYSTEMS

The best place to start is with a Business Planning System, with action items and deadlines that are constantly monitored and adhered to. You may also want to implement weekly team and management meetings, to plan for the period ahead and deal with any issues before they become major crises.

Another important system relates to your staff, and these are Key Performance Indicators. Getting this evaluation system in place is crucial, as it allows you and your employees to measure their progress against set criteria on a regular basis. Finally, it's a good idea to establish systems that monitor your budget and target goals, with regular monitoring built into the program.

## FINANCIAL SYSTEMS

Financial Systems include policies and procedures for things such as:

- ✔ Cash flow forecasts
- ✔ Sales and expense budgets
- ✔ Paying creditors and operating expenses
- ✔ Authorising expenditure
- ✔ Banking
- ✔ Petty cash
- ✔ Management reporting
- ✔ Payment of commissions and wages
- ✔ Debtor's collection

## IT SYSTEMS

Most of us rely heavily on computers and other technology in our businesses, so it's important to make sure that you have all of your IT Systems documented. Take special care to note the procedures for dealing with technology breakdowns: who are your service providers, what are their contact numbers, and what information does the company need to know about your equipment if and when you call?

## MARKETING SYSTEMS & YOUR DATABASE

This is all about measuring and tracking your marketing activities. Keep marketing analysis sheets for each campaign that show your marketing expenditure and results. By testing various marketing campaigns and comparing results, you can work out which strategies work best. You may also want to consider tracking all contact with your clients to see how often they buy from you, who your most profitable clients are, and which products or services are your most profitable.

We learnt early in our transition from technicians to business managers that our client database was one of our most important assets.

We wondered, why are we spending thousands of dollars marketing to new clients outside of our existing database, when we have a goldmine of potential clients sitting within it?

The time and money invested into the growth and maintenance of our database was definitely a Balance Sheet investment rather than a Profit & Loss expense, as the returns have come back to us many times over.

The key to success is a combination of growing your client base both inside and outside of your database but, in order to get there, you need to first and foremost ensure that your own house is in order.

We began this process by investing in the quality of information held on file. To do this we 'cleaned' our databases by ensuring that all of the contact details were correct, especially the email addresses, as email is the cheapest and easiest form of communication. Once we had this basic information right, we could then communicate regularly with our clients via email.

We then set about creating profiles of our clients so that we could send targeted, relevant information to each client depending on their particular interests. This was all about ensuring that the right information was directed to the right client.

As part of this profiling process, we began searching for detailed personal information about each client. For instance, do they own an investment property? Is their superannuation held in a managed fund or a self-managed super fund? What is their level of income? Are they business owners?

We knew that sending information about running a small business to a client who was a PAYG employee would be a waste of time, because the information is not applicable to them or their situation. The client could then become frustrated that we've wasted their time with irrelevant information.

However, if we knew that a client owned an investment property, it would make sense to communicate relevant information on topics such as land tax, changes to property tax legislation and updates from the ATO.

Essentially, we began to communicate information to each client based on their personal situation so that the content we sent them was directly useful. We no longer had a 'shotgun' approach to marketing, and although this targeted process took more time and energy to implement, the results were far better than our previous mass-marketing efforts.

Of course, to understand the real value of any marketing campaign, it's important to measure and monitor the results of the communication sent to the database. Ideally, the system you install should be able to provide you with data on readership open rates, so you can work out what is working and what is not.

You also need to manage 'bounce backs' — which is IT speak for emails that weren't delivered, as the email address wasn't valid

so that you can ensure that your database is up to date. If you're putting all of this effort into creating effective communication campaigns, you want to be sure that your message is getting through. Consequently, managing your database is an ongoing project.

## THE SECRET TO SUCCESS

Successful businesses have a number of characteristics in common, but the most prominent is the ability to deliver consistent, timely and high quality products and services. This isn't an accident. Successful businesses know that in order to attract new customers — and keep their existing customers coming back for more — they must be able to repeat the same level of service time after time.

Take McDonald's, for instance. Despite what you may think about the food, the service is always the same, regardless of whether you're in Melbourne or Moscow. That means that no matter where you travel to, your experience at McDonald's will always be consistent. McDonald's has been able to achieve this by implementing systems — including checklists, policies and procedures — that enable the company to meet its customers' expectations on every visit.

While an accounting practice may be about as far from flipping burgers as you can get, we realised that it was possible to learn from McDonald's and use some of its strategies within our own business. The McDonald's model didn't come about on day one — it took many years of trial and error before it hit on the current winning formula. McDonald's now has checklists and procedures that not only work for the business, but also for the individual.

What does this mean? In simple terms, it means that the checklists and procedures are written in such a way that everyone in the business — from the 15-year-old who has taken on their first job, to the franchise owner who runs the place — is able to understand and apply them with ease.

Of course, making burgers is a lot easier than completing a complex tax return, building a house, engineering a road or running a medical centre. But ask yourself this: if checklists and procedures can benefit a simple process, how can they be used to make complex tasks easier?

One of the key benefits of checklists and procedures is that they make complex tasks simpler to complete. For example, flying a plane is a highly complex job and pilots have checklists for every aspect of the flight. The step-by-step instructions and prompts help them to remember important information and break down even the most complex task into logical, easy-to-follow steps. Essentially, checklists take the guesswork out of the process.

In order to make checklists work for you, you'll need to follow a few simple guidelines:

- Most importantly — use them regularly! Checklists will only work for you when you use them as they have been designed.

- Get involved in the drafting of new checklists and procedures. That way, you can ensure they will be practical and will actually work.

- If you don't understand a step or instruction in a checklist, then ask! By asking, rather than interpreting or making assumptions, you will clarify the point and ensure the checklist works for you.

- Where an instruction is unclear or is open to interpretation, suggest a change to make understanding easier. That way, you'll help make the checklist work for everyone in your team.

- Keep up to date with any changes to checklists. If a change is made, make sure you're familiar with the 'what' and 'why' of the change.

- Where possible, avoid keeping your 'personal' copies of checklists and procedures. When you access these, use the versions stored in your central system — that way you can always be certain you are using the most current or 'official' version.

Finally, try to look at checklists and procedures from the right perspective. Attitude has a lot to do with making checklists that work for you. Instead of seeing them as extra red tape, a waste of time or beneath someone of your experience, consider them your work 'seat belt' — an essential safety measure that offers you a level of protection should things go wrong.

Transforming your job into a business means that everyone works together. By implementing standard checklists and procedures, duplication and bottlenecks are eliminated, which creates greater consistency.

## HOW SYSTEMS ADD VALUE

There are no two ways about it: systems add significantly to the overall value of your business.

In any business, you have limited amount of time, energy, people, resources and money. The purpose of developing systems is that you will be able to operate in the most efficient and effective way possible, in order to generate consistent results and outcomes.

When you have systems in place, your business is no longer fully dependent on you and your skills. As a result, your business will become a moneymaking machine, capable of running independently of you, and thus it will have a much higher value upon sale.

## IMPLEMENTING THE RIGHT SYSTEMS

Okay, we now understand the importance of systems. The next question is, how can you implement these systems into your business — especially when you're already working 100 hours a week as it is?!

We made the decision to employ more people in our business so they could help us get the work done and ultimately replace us, which meant we would have more time to work **on** the business.

Initially this was a very difficult decision to make, as we knew that cash flow was tight. The income that we were generating was only just supporting us as the business owners, and now we had to stretch it so it could support other people too. We had to take a financial hit and a reduction in our own personal return, so that we could re-invest. But our feeling was that we had to take one step back to take two steps forward.

We emphasis again that the important point to note here is that through the re-education process, we realised that hiring a new team member wasn't a cost but an investment. We were transitioning our mindset from technicians to managers, and when viewed from this perspective, the decision to hire was an easy one.

Once we had employed the right team members we began documenting everything we did on a day-to-day basis. In the early days we kept the process very simple by creating hard copy files for each division of the business, such as Administration, Operations, Marketing and Human Resources etc. We would then write out a process for each function in the business, and as we progressed through each function, we created a checklist (if required) and placed that into the respective files.

Next, we began systemising the processes and procedures that existed within our business. We held training sessions with our staff members on everything from how to open and close the office, and how to answer a telephone call, through to how to prepare an income tax return. We created an operations manual in hard copy and handed this to every member of the team, and instructed them to use it as their working "Bible".

Absolutely everything we did in the course of running the business was documented, and we noticed an amazing statistic: as we implemented each system and trained the team, our workload decreased — even though the business was still growing at a strong rate. This phenomenon is illustrated in the graph below:

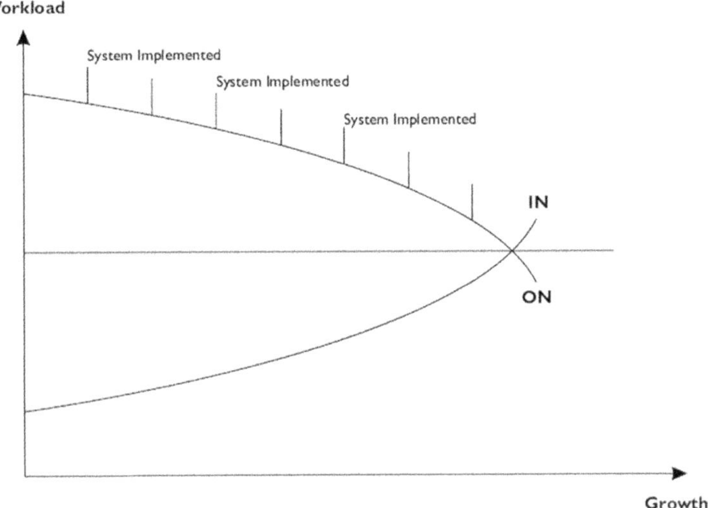


As each new system, procedure and checklist was designed, we made sure that we trained the team on how to follow the new process. Once they were trained, we were completely free from having to personally undertake this task. Instead, we simply had to manage the staff to make sure that the task was being done, rather than do the work ourselves.

At this stage we realised that we would need to develop one central area to store all of our systems so that we could maintain quality control and ensure that when a change was made, everyone in the office was up to speed on the new procedure.

Initially we were using a hard copy operations manual, but we eventually found that the manual was difficult to keep current, as we had to manage each staff member to make sure that they routinely updated their manual.

This is how the Chan & Naylor intranet was established in its first humble incarnation. The intranet is basically an internal system that can be accessed by all staff members. This became our 'hub' where we stored all of our systems, procedures, policies and checklists. As a result, our operations manual become a live, working document that was updated regularly and was accessible by all staff on their own computers at a moment's notice.

The intranet provided a huge benefit to us, as it meant that we only had to update our operations manual in one place when a change was made. This system unexpectedly became a whole new business for us, as other accountants and business owners saw the benefit of what we had created. We set about creating a commercial product and another business was launched from this simple idea... but that's another story!

These days, we now spend around 80% of our time on preventative measures, which has reduced the number of 'fires' that needed to be attended to. The more we work **on** the business, the less we have to work **in** the business. Working on the business involves creating systems and training people, which in turn means that less involvement is required from us as the Partners.

We have found that over time, our systems and our people have begun to do the work that we used to do — and we now have a business that works, so that we have choice.

PART 8

# The Importance of Culture

Chan & Naylor today is a successful, growing business that is no longer reliant on the founding owners to operate. The business generates passive income streams for us both, and we continue to choose to work as we view it as a challenge. We sit on the various Boards of the many businesses we have helped to create, and we only spend our time working in the strategic areas of the business and mentoring our partners.

The journey to this point hasn't been easy, however, the one major realisation we've had is the importance of culture. A major part of the success of Chan & Naylor, and most other successful organisations, is the culture and core values that have been instilled, as these form the fabric of the organisation.

Chan & Naylor has grown tremendously over the past two decades and we know that the fundamental culture that underpins the business has been instrumental in its success.

The word 'culture' is bandied around a lot in organisations without any real understanding of what the term means. At Chan & Naylor, culture simply refers to 'the way we do things around here'. When creating a business that works so you don't have to, we believe that it's critical to establish your values and follow through.

The values that we've applied to our business as our basic Code of Conduct were nothing more than standard, socially accepted values and common courtesy, such as:

- ✔ Act with honesty in all dealings with team members and clients/customers
- ✔ Act with integrity and professionalism at all times
- ✔ Always show respect to others by acknowledging and communicating

- ✔ Always return calls and respond to correspondence promptly
- ✔ Speak to each other politely using a person's name — using please and thank you at a minimum
- ✔ Greet and farewell everyone in a positive, cheerful way
- ✔ Blame a system, not a person
- ✔ Own a problem until you're sure that the appropriate person has taken over this problem
- ✔ If you have a problem with someone, talk about the problem only with them in private — don't gossip

These values are important to us and they're vital to the success of our business. Consequently, when a new staff member joins the team, this is the message that they receive on their first day:

***CHAIRMAN'S WELCOME***

I would like to take this opportunity to welcome you to the Chan & Naylor family and wish you every success with your new adventure, because your success is our success.

We have an open door policy because we believe that you should work in a safe environment, where you can express concerns or provide us with feedback that enables us to resolve blockages and bring about a free-flowing organisation.

***MISSION STATEMENT & GUARANTEE***

I'd also like to take this opportunity to mention some very important things. I've attached our Mission Statement and our 12 Point Guarantee, which I want you to read.

One of the things that has made Chan & Naylor such a success in the community is our willingness to help our clients and each other.

This willingness has seen clients give our firm a 93.8% rating for 'good to excellent' service, year in, year out. We are very proud of this record and protect it fearlessly and enforce it strongly.

This culture begins with our willingness to be respectful to others in our communication with them. Fundamental to this great record is our attitude to our clients' needs, which begins with our responsiveness to their emails and phone calls.

We take our 12 Point Guarantee very seriously.You will note that Point 4 talks about our guarantee "to return emails and phone calls within 24 hours". In practice, I expect this to occur within the same day, but at the very least it should not be longer than the next day, allowing for meetings and delays.

If we do the very basic things that our parents taught us, which simply constitutes good manners, we cannot help but be successful. It's generally the little things that create the biggest problems — so let's do the basic things well, and success will automatically follow.

### ***ANSWERING EMAILS & PHONE CALLS***

The above guarantee also extends to a very important policy that we follow here at Chan & Naylor, which is as follows.

I want to make it very clear to everyone that I expect everyone to reply to emails and return calls promptly. Promptly means preferably within the same day but no later than the next day.

Most, if not all, emails require a simple response such as "will do" to indicate that you understand and acknowledge the person who has sent it. If everybody follows these principles it will make all of our jobs much easier, especially for the Client Managers and Partners.

In this day and age, communication is fast and swift. Our business will expand only to the degree that we answer and reply to our communication. Our clients and fellow staff members constantly rate us based on the relevance and speed of our communication. Therefore, the above policy must be followed and only relevant communication should be sent. Keep that in mind and you'll be fast, efficient and you'll expand along with the organisation.

***YOUR TURN***

With that said, I hope that your stay at Chan & Naylor is rewarding and challenging. My only request from you is that you reply to this email and let me know what your thoughts are on the information provided, including our Mission Statement and Guarantee. And I want your solemn promise that you will reply to emails and communication swiftly.

I look forward to your reply.

* * * *

New staff members are also provided with a copy of our Mission Statement and Peace of Mind Guarantee on their first day, so that they're aware of the culture that our business promotes.

## THE SCIENCE OF CULTURE

The culture at Chan & Naylor didn't develop overnight; we spent several years figuring out what worked and what didn't. We also applied some science to the process, and we'd like to share our findings with you and explain how they apply practically.

The principles, which will be discussed in later chapters, are as follows:

- Work with the 80/20 principle
- Think Win/Win — the concept of fair exchange
- Scarcity versus abundance
- Understand the principles of time management and being 'effective' rather than just 'efficient'
- Build relationships and trust
- See things from the other person's point of view

- Under-promise and over-deliver

These principles or core values of our organisation have nothing to do with the technical nature of our business; they are more to do with a person's morals, or their soft or interpersonal skills.

All of our team members are inducted into the organisation and these principles are taught and reinforced through ongoing education, training and practical day-to-day examples. The language becomes part of daily operations and the team lives and breathes it. In the following chapters, we will explain these principles in detail and how they apply to your business.

## THE 80/20 RULE

This is a principle that is entrenched in the culture of Chan & Naylor, and we believe that every business owner should understand this concept and how it applies to their organisation.

In 1906, Italian economist Vilfredo Pareto created a mathe- matical formula to describe the unequal distribution of wealth in his country. He observed that 20% of the people owned 80% of the land. After Pareto made his observation and created his formula, many others observed similar phenomena in their own areas of expertise.

Dr. Joseph Juran was working in the US in the 1930s and 1940s when he recognised a universal principle that he called the "vital few and trivial many".

In his early work, a lack of precision on Juran's part made it appear like he was applying Pareto's observations about economics to a broader body of work, and the name 'Pareto's Principle' stuck — probably because it sounded better than Juran's Principle.

As a result, Dr. Juran's observation of the "vital few and trivial many" — which is the principle that 20% of something is always responsible for 80% of the results — became forever known as Pareto's Principle, or the 80/20 rule.

The 80/20 rule means that in any situation, a few (20%) are vital and many (80%) are trivial. In Pareto's case, it meant 20% of the people owned 80% of the land. In Juran's initial work, he identified that 20% of the defects caused 80% of the problems.

Project managers know that 20% of the work (the first 10% and the last 10%) consumes 80% of their time and resources. You can apply the 80/20 rule to almost anything, from the science of management to the physical world.

Let's see, then, how Pareto's Principle works in our practical lives. If you think about it, you generally wear 20% of your clothes 80% of the time, and 80% of your clothes are worn only 20% of the time. You may associate with 20% of your friends 80% of the time, and the remaining 80% of your friends you see only 20% of the time. You use 20% of your cutlery 80% of the time — and we all have our favourite mug that we use daily!

In the business arena, it is often believed that 80% of your business income is generated by 20% of your client base, while 20% of your customers create 80% of your problems.

It may also be the case that 20% of your stock takes up 80% of your warehouse space; 80% of your sales will be generated by 20% of your sales staff; 20% of your team create 80% of your problems, and so on and so on. We undertook this exercise with our own business and the numbers did show that this was the case.

When we first understood this principle, we began to apply it to our day-to-day activities in the way that we did things at Chan & Naylor. Shortly thereafter, our team started to understand how the 80/20 rule applied to their daily lives.

What we then realised was that there is a big difference between being **efficient** and being **effective.** You could be the most productive employee and get the work in and out of the office in record time, but you still might not be working effectively.

We also realised that by being the technician and doing the actual work or producing the product or service, we only achieved 20% of the overall result, even though it consumed 80% of our time to do this. This was another example of being efficient without being effective.

## EFFICIENCY VS. EFFECTIVENESS

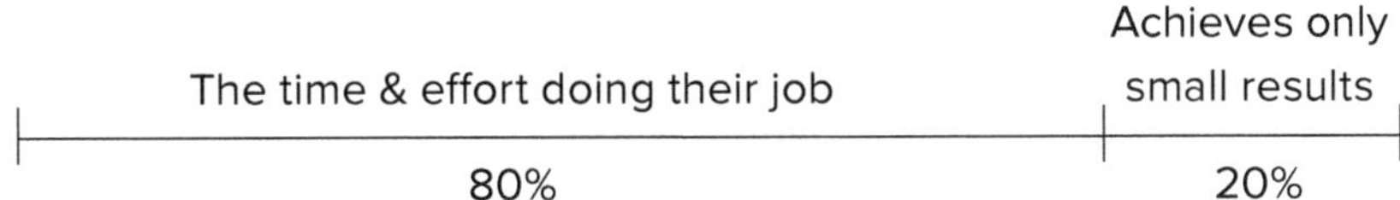


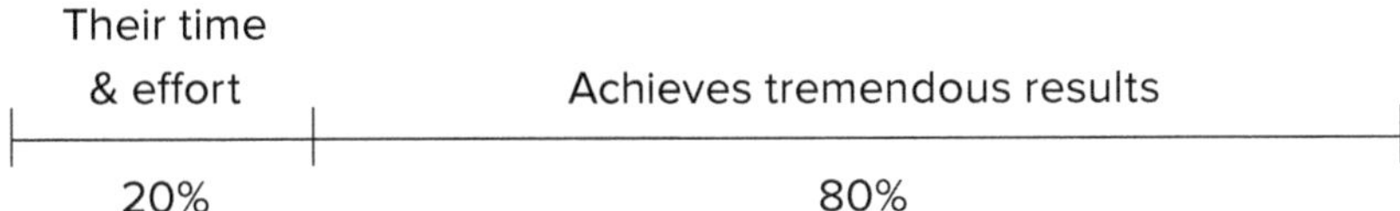


By developing systems and training our employees on various processes and policies, particularly on interpersonal skills, we found that they became much more effective.

For example, when producing a product or a service for the client, the actual completion of the work takes 80% of the time, but it really has only a 20% result from a client's point of view. However, the delivery of the product or service — such as how the customer or client is communicated to — requires just 20% of the overall effort, but it achieves a massive 80% result.

Let's look at a practical example. When you purchase a new car from a showroom, the sales person takes you for a test drive, discusses the features and benefits of the vehicle in detail, walks you through the customer service facilities, manages the handover and generally follows up after you leave the showroom.

While it takes several months to build a quality motor vehicle, the purchasing process may have taken just a few hours. However, the result of those few hours and your experience with the sales person and the company determines your overall impression of your car buying experience.

If the sales person is effective in this process, it achieves 80% of the result by selling you the car — yet it has taken only 20% of the overall time involved in producing, marketing and selling the car to achieve this outcome.

For those in a service industry, let's look at another example. Let's say you are running the service and repair department of the car dealership. You spend 10 hours working on the repair and servicing of a customer's car and you do this very efficiently, exerting 80% of your effort with this particular client on their car.

The other 20% of effort involved in this transaction is spent dealing with the client, explaining exactly what needs to be fixed, asking permission to proceed with repairs and on conclusion, explaining what you have done to the car. This communication with the customer produces 80% of the result, as you need their input and responses to proceed with the work.

If you want to create an effective **and** efficient business, you must understand this principle. Just as importantly, you need to ensure that your staff understands it as well.

## WIN/WIN OR FAIR EXCHANGE

The Win/Win philosophy, or the concept of fair exchange, has been an integral part of our culture from the very outset of Chan & Naylor. For a business to succeed, all major stakeholders must benefit or profit from the relationship — not just the owners.

The major stakeholders of a business include:

1. The owners or shareholders
2. The staff or team members
3. The creditors or suppliers
4. The customers or clients

In order for a business to be successful, all of the various stakeholders need to experience a 'win' in the relationship. The shareholders must receive a return on their investment. The staff must be remunerated fairly and have challenging and rewarding roles. The creditors or suppliers must be paid promptly for their product or service. And of course, the client or customer must receive a quality end product or service at a reasonable and fair price.

## WIN/WIN

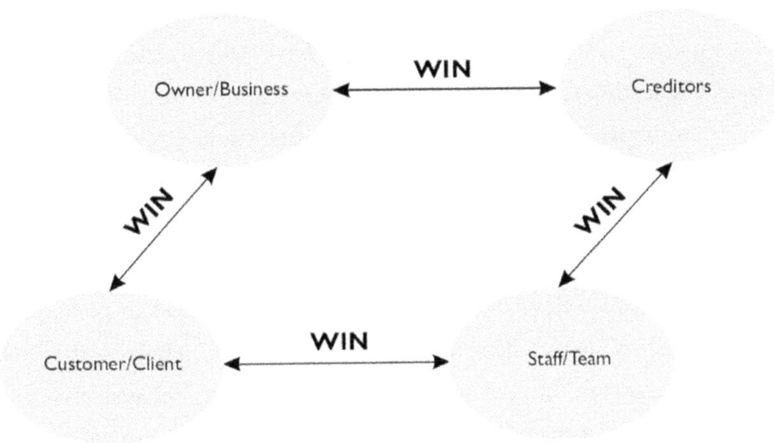


If anyone in the chain above loses, it could have a detrimental impact on the operation of your organisation.

## SCARCITY VS ABUNDANCE

In previous chapters, we've talked about the importance of your staff and the different personality types that exist within your organisation. There is no 'right' or 'wrong' personality type; we have each been given different personalities for a purpose. But if you are truly going to be able to leverage your business, you must ensure that you surround yourself with what we call 'Abundant' people.

An Abundant person is someone who understands that they must give first in order to receive something in return. For example, they produce a product or result and receive remuneration in return. They give first and then expect to receive, and they understand the win/win concept of fair exchange.

We define a 'Scarcity' person as someone who expects to receive something, but they don't necessarily produce anything or perform any tasks in exchange for this. For example, in our society we acknowledge that social security for people in legitimate need is essential, however, society has indirectly created many Scarcity-minded people who believe that society owes them a living. They become conditioned to expect to receive social security in the form of unemployment benefits, without having to produce anything in return — and this expectation becomes the standard, rather than the exception.

As a business owner, how many times have you had a staff member approach you asking for an increase in remuneration? Of course, they should be well remunerated in the first instance, and in some circumstances your employee may be able to demonstrate why they deserve a pay rise.

But others simply want more. They don't understand the concept of win/win and, as a result, they can be a drain on your energy and resources.

Over the years we have dealt with many different types of personalities and we can tell you for a fact that Scarcity people are much more difficult to manage. They don't fit into the culture of Chan & Naylor because our culture is win/win, so these types of people eventually leave the organisation.

It is even more vital that your management team and partners are Abundant people, as these types of people are ultimately responsible for the success of your business. We have made the mistake of going into business with Scarcity people in the past and none of these ventures have been successful, so we have learnt from our mistakes and now choose to work only with Abundant personalities.

When we induct a new team member at Chan & Naylor, we educate them on all of these principles — and whenever a staff member seeks a salary review, they are aware that there has to be a win involved for each of the stakeholders.

For example, when a team member asks for a pay increase, we ask: how will this benefit the stakeholders? If we increase their salary, an instant impact will be felt, as profits will be reduced, which may in turn impact on suppliers because of cash flow. If the shareholders' profits are to be maintained, the business may have to increase its prices to the client or customer, and if these prices aren't in line with the market, the client could leave. If the client leaves, the income stops, and consequently everyone loses their jobs.

If the owner simply gives the pay increase to the staff member without fair exchange, the owners are in a lose/win situation. This is a Scarcity mindset and will not work. On the other hand, if the staff member doesn't get a pay rise, they may see this as a lose/win situation, and you may very well lose a key member of your team.

If you imagine your business as if it were a pie, you can see that it's set at a certain size. When someone wants a bigger slice of the pie in the form of a pay rise, someone else usually ends up with a smaller slice of the pie as a result. So what is one to do?

The Abundant solution is to increase the size of the overall pie, so that everyone can access a larger slice. There are strategies you can use to accomplish this, such as putting in place incentives that reward employees when productivity increases. Abundant people focus on increasing the size of the pie, which in turn leads to better conditions and wages. Scarcity people are only interested in getting a larger slice of the pie without increasing productivity or better conditions for everyone involved.

When a staff member does approach you for a pay increase, you need to work through a solution that creates a win/win solution for all parties and focus their attention on remuneration based on productivity and profits.

These could be as follows:

1. Create a bonus system to allow the team member to achieve their increase, but only if they achieve certain targets and productivity levels.

2. Award the pay increase, but only if the team member takes on more responsibility and becomes accountable for higher levels of production.

3. Ensure that the employee is being paid fairly as per market expectations, and create a system whereby all staff members share in the profits of the business by offering a form of employee share arrangement.

**Chan and Naylor profit share bonus systems** are based on production and not discretion. If certain goals and targets are achieved by a member of our team, then they will be rewarded with a share in the firm's profits… We have a culture of rewarding results, not just effort.

Here is a bonus process and some ideas you may consider for your small business:

1. Firstly Partners, owners and Boards must determine how much of profits they are prepared to set aside for bonuses. This is based on forward cash flow and budgetary requirements of the business, taking into account win/win for all stakeholders. For instance, **shareholders** must receive a return on investment, and cash flow/reserves must be maintained to ensure **creditors and suppliers** are paid. Your **team is** rewarded for personal exertion via salaries and wages that should meet market expectation.

2. You then need to set a performance target to trigger entitlement to the bonus.

3. The first trigger to be entitled to a bonus is to set an achievable overall profit or EBIT (Earnings Before Interest and Tax) target for your business. First and foremost, the business must achieve this overall goal. This target needs to be communicated to all team members from the outset, and more importantly, reiterated on a regular basis to manage expectations. These targets need to be achievable and measured against generally acceptable industry KPI's with the aim to be at the upper level or beyond. For example, the industry standard profit benchmarks or EBIT expected for the accounting industry is around 30-40%. Other industries have standard benchmarks and this data is easily accessible through respective industry groups.

4. If the overall business profit target has been achieved by the business, this triggers access to the bonus. The next step is to determine the distribution of the bonus amongst the team, which can be either based on individual performance or team performance, dependant on the internal structure of your business. Their profit share is calculated by their respective contributions to the achievement of reaching the overall profit/ EBIT target of the business. It may be the case that even though the business has reached its overall target, some individuals or teams do not reach their individual targets. We have a scale of achievement with a minimum level, which means that if the firm has hit its overall target

and yet an individual or team has not, they can still share in a profit, albeit at a lower rate. This is why regular communication throughout the period to help, mentor and assist your team as they work towards reaching their targets is so important.

5. To calculate the individual or team contribution to the overall profit (and therefore their entitlement to the share of the bonus), you need to treat each team or individual as a "profit centre". Start by working through the KPI on what was their contribution to sales or revenue, **less** the fixed overhead such as **direct wages,** and then allocate a percentage of **the variable business** overhead. Our formulae of allocating overhead is by working out total fixed costs and dividing this figure by the amount of income-producing staff within each respective team

6. Individual or team bonuses are based on their performance. For example, if a team or individual has only achieved 25% profit and another individual or team 45% profit, then the first team would share in less of the bonus. You should have a set, pre-determined scale and formula to work this out.

7. If you have a team bonus structure, you also have to predetermine the percentage on how to split the bonus amongst that respective team. This process is discretionaryandeachbusinesswillneedtoworkthrough a system that is fair and equitable, in our business the best way to do this is based on our understanding of the roles within the team, for example, the senior manager has a lot more responsibility and larger workload than a junior clerk or support member — and therefore, the share of the bonus should be weighted accordingly. You will also come across situations where a staff member leaves during a bonus period, you may want to apply discretion here however we have a policy that bonuses are forfeited on a staff member leaving.

## EXAMPLE OF BONUS CALCULATIONS

Let's assume the business profit target figure to trigger profit share is 35%.

Sales for the year were $500,000, less expenses of $300,000 EBIT (Net earnings of business before interest and tax) of $200,000 = 40% **trigger reached**

Let's assume there are two teams. Team 1's contribution to revenue was $300,000, Team 2's contribution to revenue was $200,000.

| **eBIT Calculation Team 1** | **$** | |
|---|---|---|
| Actual revenue generated | 300,000 | |
| Less Wages | 100,000 | |
| Less Overheads | 50,000 | |
| Profit Team 1 | 150,000 | |
| eBIT for team | 50% | If less than 25% no bonus paid |
| | | |
| **Bonus distribution Calculation for Team 1** | | |
| If 25% EBIT achieved | 5.0% | - |
| If 30% EBIT achieved | 7.5% | - |
| If 35% EBIT achieved | 10.0% | |
| If 40% plus EBIT achieved | 12.5% | 18,750 |
| Bonus Allocation | | 18,750 |
| | | |
| **Distribution of Bonus amongst Team 1** | | |
| Senior Manager/ salesperson % of Bonus | 60% | 11,250 |
| Admin/Support % of Bonus | 40% | 7,500 |
| **Total** | | **18,750** |

| **eBIT Calculation Team 2** | | |
|---|---|---|
| Actual revenue generated | 200,000 | |
| Less Wages | 100,000 | |
| Less Overheads | 50,000 | |
| **Profit Team 2** | 50,000 | |
| **eBIT for team** | **25%** | If less than 25% no bonus paid. |
| | | |
| **Bonus distribution Calculation for Team 2** | | |
| If 25% EBIT achieved | 5.0% | 2,500 |
| If 30% EBIT achieved | 7.5% | - |
| If 35% EBIT achieved | 10.0% | |
| If 40% plus EBIT achieved | 12.5% | |
| **Bonus Allocation** | | **2,500** |
| | | |
| **Distribution of Bonus amongst Team 2** | | |
| Senior Manager/ salesperson % of Bonus | 60% | 1,500 |
| Admin/Support % of Bonus | 40% | 1,000 |
| **Total** | | **2,500** |

There are always challenges when formulating a bonus or profit share system that suits your business and the individuals within, and the ideas above are just examples of what has worked for us. There are many variations to this, and the above strategy may not necessary work for you.

However, what we have found (although there are always exceptions) is that in order to take emotion away from the debate, you need to take discretion away from bonus systems calculations, and instead rely on a pre-determined system.

You also need to communicate this to your team so they all know the rules they are playing by upfront. Always be mindful that even though you place a system in for a given year, this system might not work for you or your team, so be flexible as you reassess, adapt and reintroduce and test an improved strategy the following year.

### *PROMOTE FROM WITHIN*

As your business grows and you step further away from the daily functions, the culture of the organisation may come under threat. After all, you are passing on these tasks and responsibilities to other people, so you are relying on them to use the same philosophies that you use.

The basic fundamentals of our culture are not complicated and are nothing more than standard, socially accepted values and common courtesy. They are easy to learn and easy to follow, and they're simple enough to be carried on from generation to generation.

Many managers and business owners believe that it's better to promote staff from within the organisation, as these people have been 'brought up' living the culture and understand 'how we do it around here'. If the appropriate people are available within your organisation to promote, then this can be a good strategy.

However, in the early stages of developing your business, you may need to recruit resources and skill-sets from outside of your organisation in order to take your business to the next level and achieve leverage.

By bringing in a fresh perspective, you will gain a staff member that has his or her own belief system and opinions. Some of these may clash with your organisation's culture and philosophies, but the trick here is to make sure that the core fabrics of the culture remain valued. Provided that you have a solid recruitment system in place to ensure that the person will 'fit in' and you provide ongoing training, you can still maintain these standards, even with clashing personality types.

As the business develops and grows, you will generally have a group of people called the Board of Directors who ensure that the culture continues to flourish and be maintained. The Board is often comprised of owners and key stakeholders who have been brought up in the system and who understand the need to maintain the corporate culture. Generally, the chairman works very closely with the managing director to ensure that the core culture is followed throughout the organisation.

## COMMUNICATION IN THE MODERN ERA

How you communicate with your staff and your clients/ customers forms an important part of your business's culture.

When we first started our business, in the days before mobile phones and email, computers were huge, cumbersome boxes that took up a lot of space and processed information very slowly. We did a lot of our work manually by preparing financial accounts on large manual spreadsheets and handwriting tax returns.

When we wanted to communicate with a staff member, client or supplier, we simply picked up the phone and talked, or we arranged a face-to-face meeting. We had regular staff meetings and distributed memos and spoke to people individually. Our employees didn't have computers and many of our clients didn't either, as technology had yet to deliver email and text messaging.

Advances in communications technology led to the mobile phone, which became an essential part of working life. Then along came email, which made communicating even easier faster and more efficient than ever before...

But there is a big difference between being efficient and being effective. Although email may have made communicating faster and more efficient for all stakeholders, it hasn't necessarily made communicating more effective, as it relies on the skills of the individual. This is why we spend many hours training staff to communicate effectively.

How many times have you received an email communication from someone, either internally within your office or from a client or supplier, and you've taken offence? Before you know it, out of anger and emotion, you've tapped away at your computer keyboard and created a terse email in response — and then they reply, and on it goes...

We've all done it before, but when we learnt that this wasn't the best way to deal with an issue, we created a policy to address it. At Chan & Naylor, if a problem arises between staff members or with a client, and communication is taking place via email, we move the conversation offline. We ensure that we pick up the phone or have a meeting and talk to the people directly involved.

When handled this way, the result is usually completely different. In fact, in many cases, it is discovered that the original emailer had not intended to upset or offend the recipient. Perhaps the email was read out of context, or the wording/tone was open to interpretation. Regardless, all of the people involved have wasted countless hours of productive time dealing with this issue, which could have been avoided with more effective communication.

Over the years we have experienced many situations where one person has sent an email and the recipient has interpreted the email in a different context than was intended. On other occasions, the sender has intended to cause a reaction, but they have inflamed the situation by relying on email — where only words tell the story, without the benefit of tone, body language and off-the-cuff conversation.

In today's modern society, it is sometimes easier to hide behind an email than to deal with an issue head-on, and many people have lost the skill of communicating via phone or face to face. This can be a dangerous habit to have your organisation fall into.

You may have noticed in recent times that many of the service industries, such as banks, are reverting back to an older model of face-to-face contact and communication with their clients. Some have even gone as far as advertising the faces and names of bank managers, and many of them advertise the fact that when you call them, you will speak to a "real person" rather than an automated service.

They are doing this because they see it as a point of difference, and they believe that offering strong levels of customer service will give them a competitive edge.

We have a policy in our organisation that if you need to address an issue or problem internally or externally, you must pick up the phone and call the other person directly, rather than sending an email or text. Yes, it is easier and sometimes more efficient to send an email, and it certainly feels less confrontational, but you must instil these skills in your team. The ability to handle difficult situations head-on is much more effective.

When used correctly, emails are a fantastic tool and they undeniably form part of the modern working environment. They have made communicating a much easier process. But it pays to be aware that when emails are not utilised correctly, they can become a non-productive, less effective form of communication.

As directors of the Board and business owners, we have occasionally written emails in anger, emotion and frustration, so we now have a personal policy to not send any emails we're unsure of. Instead, we leave it 24 hours and revisit the email the following day. If you follow this same philosophy, you will probably find that once the emotion is gone, you will pick up the phone and deal with the person directly, or you will change the context of the email. In many ways, the first draft acts as a form of release — and you have to remember that as the owner of a business, conflict resolution is part and parcel of your job.

The rule that all of our staff at Chan & Naylor follow is, if in doubt, take a deep breath and re-read the email, taking into account the other person's point of view. This needs to be done before you click the send button, because more often than not, you can't take it back!

**PART 9**

# Time Management

One of the most important principles that all small business owners should understand and apply is the principle of time management.

Once you understand the benefits of time management and apply the principle to your day-to-day working life, you can then train and educate your team to do the same. This will make a tremendous difference to the way your business functions and how, where and when you, as the owner, are able to leverage your time.

Time is one of our most important resources, and what we do with it over our lifetime is critical, as it determines whether we will be successful or not.

In his book *The 7 Habits of Highly Effective People,* Dr Stephen R Covey discusses his theory that our time is generally broken into four quadrants. We touched on this briefly in Chapter 4. The four quadrants are:

Quadrant I = Activity that is Urgent and Important Quadrant II = Activity that is not Urgent, but is Important Quadrant III = Activity that is not Important, but is Urgent Quadrant IV = Activity that is not Urgent and not Important

Covey proposes the Time Management Matrix, which more clearly outlines his theory:

| | Urgent | Not urgent |
|---|---|---|
| **Important** | **QUADRANT I**<br>Urgent/Important<br>Characterised by: Crises<br>Pressing problems<br>Deadlines | **QUADRANT II**<br>Important/Not Urgent<br>Characterised by:<br>Planning Prevention<br>Relationship building |
| **Not Important** | **QUADRANT III**<br>Urgent/Not Important<br>Characterised by:<br>Interruptions Mail,<br>reports Some meetings | **QUADRANT IV**<br>Not Important/Not Urgent<br>Characterised by:<br>Trivia Time wasters<br>Busy work |

### *QUADRANT I — IMPORTANT/URGENT*

This is all about working **in** your business. Quadrant I is characterised by matters that require immediate attention and have significant results. For instance, a ringing phone is a Quadrant I activity because it will generally take precedence over other matters. This Quadrant is also about reacting to problems when they arise and putting out fires, because problems are important and urgent.

A business owner who works in Quadrant I all the time is unlikely to build the successful business that they desire, simply because most of their time and energy is dedicated to dealing with one problem after the next and putting out fires. The end result is excessive stress and eventual burnout.

In our industry, this is akin to the senior partner preparing income tax returns for the clients, rather than hiring other qualified accountants to take care of this work. It is both important and urgent that this work gets done, otherwise you will incur penalties and have irate clients, but that doesn't mean that you — as the business owner

need to be the one doing the work.

### QUADRANT II — IMPORTANT/NOT URGENT

This is about working **on** your business, and really it is about prevention and planning. Quadrant II is the ideal place to spend most of your time. In Quadrant II you have a long-term focus and you're planning for the future by anticipating issues and putting procedures in place to deal with matters before they arise. In the example above, for instance, rather than the partner completing income tax returns for clients (a Quadrant I activity), he or she would be better off developing checklists and systems and hiring and training staff, so that they can do the work instead.

In the business setting, Quadrant II activities include maintaining the database, training staff, developing training manuals and establishing recruitment processes, as these are all tasks that prevent problems from occurring in the future.

Although the activities in this quadrant may not be urgent, you're essentially preventing fires by anticipating issues before they happen. Those business owners who work in Quadrant II have personal control, enjoy few crises in their businesses and lead more balanced lives.

### QUADRANT III — URGENT/NOT IMPORTANT

Quadrant III is characterised by matters that appear important, but in actual fact make no significant contribution to your goals. They will generally be someone else's priority. Business owners who work in Quadrant III are more likely to fail because they feel out of control, spend little time planning and may even consider goals to be a waste of time. Covey says people who spend time exclusively in Quadrant III "lead irresponsible lives"!

Examples of Quadrant III activities include going through spam emails or taking urgent but unimportant phone calls — such as from a sales person trying to sell you a Mini Minor at a "never to be repeated" discount when you're not even in the market for a car.

### QUADRANT IV — NOT IMPORTANT/NOT URGENT

Quadrant IV activities make no contribution towards your goals and don't require urgent attention. These are true time wasters. Business owners who operate in Quadrant IV are most likely to fail. Examples of Quadrant IV activities include idle chitchat in the office or calling/attending a one-hour meeting with no agenda, no purpose and no real outcome. People who work consistently in Quadrant IV produce very little of substance and will often rely on others to deliver results.

## WHICH QUADRANT DO YOU OPERATE IN?

Time management is a crucial skill for you and your staff members to master. To ensure that you're all making the most of your time, ask every person in your organisation to write down every single task they do in an average day. Then, ask them to categorise each item in one of the four respective quadrants.

This provides a great opportunity to evaluate where your team members are spending their time, and it won't be long before you identify ways to better redistribute their resources. If you find that your receptionist is dedicating too much time to Quadrant III and IV activities, for instance, you may be able to introduce some checklists and policies to get him or her working more efficiently in Quadrant I and II.

Managers who undertake this experiment should be able to identify any Quadrant III activities that they can delegate to someone else. They may also be able to partially or fully delegate some Quadrant I activities to other staff members (with appropriate training and guidance), as they work towards a goal of working exclusively in Quadrant II.

As business owners, the bulk of our day is often spent reacting to client and customer demands, deadlines and requests. It is possible, however, to build a business that minimises activity in Quadrant I, III and IV, and allows us to focus most of our time in Quadrant II. Quadrant II is about planning for the future. It includes preventative maintenance tasks and building strong relationships. Business owners who regularly work in Quadrant II are in control and have clear goals, so they adopt a long-term view and enjoy a balanced life. In other words, they work **on** their business rather than **in** it, and they don't spend all of their time reacting to one crisis after the next.

To build such a business, you need to set goals and prioritise activities. You can start this process by systemising your business and delegating tasks to your team members. You need to stop being **reactive** (Quadrant I activity) and start being **proactive** (Quadrant II activity) by spending time planning and learning to say "no" to activities that don't contribute to your goals.

It won't be easy because you'll have to break years of bad habits, but it can be done. You know our story; we each used to spend over 100 hours every week working in our practice, mainly on Quadrant I activities. We were burning out and had little time for our families and came home from work exhausted every night.

By using the principles of Dr Stephen R Covey and Michael Gerber, we were able to start the process of transforming our business. This meant working on some Quadrant I, III and IV activities in the early days, but once we got systems in place and delegated to our new team, we began spending more and more time in Quadrant II. These days, we spend 100% of our time in Quadrant II planning the future of our business, building relationships with our clients, service providers and strategic partners, and making sure we prevent future problems. Quadrant I activities hardly ever arise, and Quadrant IV activities are almost extinct.

## MAXIMISING YOUR TIME

To explain this concept more clearly and give you an appreciation of how it works in our daily personal lives and within our business, we'll give you some practical examples that we use during our staff training sessions.

Let's say that Tony is driving along a busy highway in peak- hour and he's in the centre lane, crawling along in bumper-to- bumper traffic. Suddenly, the engine starts spluttering and choking, and without warning it completely cuts out. Horns start blowing and traffic starts to back up behind Tony, and the whole highway comes to a standstill because his car has broken down.

Now, consider these questions. Does this situation require Tony's immediate attention, and is the situation urgent? It's extremely important that he gets this situation fixed and his car moved, so of course it is classified as both urgent and important, and therefore the activity would fit into Quadrant I.

Now let's consider an alternative scenario. This time let's assume that Tony was diligent in servicing his car every six months, and even though the car was running smoothly, he still took the time to arrange regular servicing.

Because of this regular maintenance, the car was in tip-top shape, which prevented it from breaking down.

Did the car require immediate attention when Tony booked it in for each six-month check-up? No, because it wasn't urgent at the time. However, was it important that the car was serviced? Yes, because it was a preventative measure that helped to avert an issue down the track. As a result, the activity of getting the car regularly serviced falls into Quadrant II (not urgent, but important).

Which scenario (Quadrant I or Quadrant II) was more effective in terms of time management? The answer is Quadrant II, of course, because as they say, prevention is always better than cure.

Let's take a look at another example before we start applying this to the business arena.

Rebecca has just had her backyard landscaped with beautiful and expensive flowers. The flowers require water to stay alive, so every afternoon she spends half an hour watering the flowers to enable them to flourish and grow. This activity requires immediate, urgent and regular attention, and it is important otherwise the flowers will die. Therefore, because it is urgent and important, this activity falls into Quadrant I.

However, Rebecca has done some research and has discovered that she can install a sprinkler system that automatically comes on every day and waters the garden for 30 minutes. She immediately books the installation and just one week later, she has her evenings back to herself while her garden remains nourished from the automatic watering system.

Was the installation of the automatic watering system important? Yes, most certainly. But did the research and time devoted to this require immediate, urgent attention? Not exactly, because there was always the option of continuing to water the garden by hand each day. Therefore, installing the watering system is a Quadrant II activity, as it is important but not urgent.

Are you starting to get the picture? Working in Quadrant II is all about preventing the potential issues that crop up in Quadrant

So now let's explore some examples of how this principle could apply to your business.

If you've read this far, you know by heart the difference between working **in** your business and working **on** your business. The person working in the business is the technician and they're usually applying their time to Quadrant I activities. The person working on the business is the manager, and they spend their time more effectively in Quadrant II.

As discussed in earlier chapters, when you're first starting out it can be difficult to work both in and on your business, as you're effectively working across all four quadrants.

When Chan & Naylor first launched, we were working in the business 100% of the time, dealing with all of the tasks that required urgent attention and were important. This included things such as doing the actual tax work, putting out fires with customers and answering phones.

However, as we began to understand the concept of time management, we learnt where we should be most effectively spending our time — in Quadrant II. We slowly started to devote more and more time to Quadrant II and to our surprise, we found that the more time we spent in that area, the less time we needed to spend in Quadrant I.

## WORKING IN OTHER QUADRANTS

Although it should be your goal to spend most of your time in Quadrant II, it is inevitable that you will need to spend time in the other quadrants as well. By using the principles of delegation, and implementing procedures and systems, you will be able to limit the amount of time you spend in Quadrants I, III and IV.

Quadrant III is all about tasks that are not important, but that do require urgent and immediate attention. A perfect example of this is the phone ringing — the phone needs to be answered within a short period of time, but the content of the conversation might not be urgent.

If you receive a call from a telemarketer, for instance, the shrill ring of the telephone requires your urgent attention. But when the telemarketer starts promoting a computer package, and you have just recently bought a computer, you will ascertain that the content of the phone call isn't important to you, so you're unlikely to persist with the conversation, as it is clearly a Quadrant III activity (urgent, but not important).

Quadrant IV involves time spent on activities that are neither urgent nor important, such as watching television.

The amount of time that you spend in Quadrant III and IV will vary depending on your business, but as you can see, it's clear that most of your day should be spent planning, managing and dealing with matters that make a significant contribution to your goals. In other words, you should be proactively focusing on relationships and results — not fussing about in the kitchen, or answering phones and directing calls.

The most truly effective business people eliminate the need to spend any time in Quadrant III and IV, so they can spend most of their time in Quadrant II. And what's the best way to delegate Quadrant III and IV tasks? By implementing the right systems, of course.

## MOVING TO QUADRANT II

It can be difficult to transition from working **in** the business to working **on** the business, and here's why.

Writing up and developing systems is an important task, but it does not require immediate attention, so it's not urgent. It's a Quadrant II activity.

Training your team is equally as important, but again, it's not as urgent as other tasks. Ditto for creating or updating your business plan: it is important, but when there's other work to be done to keep the dollars flowing in, it's generally acceptable practice to just get out there and do the work.

Completing the actual technical work of the business requires immediate attention and is important, otherwise the business cannot survive, so this Quadrant I activity often takes up most of your time.

The trick is to start gradually working in Quadrant II by writing up procedures and implementing systems for the basic tasks that can be delegated. Once these activities are delegated and the team member has been trained, you are then free from ever having to do that task again.

Your role now is simply to manage and to ensure the task is being completed. The more time you can spend in Quadrant II managing and streamlining, the less time you'll need to spend in Quadrant I actually doing the work.

It's important to understand that working in Quadrant II is not about ignoring urgent matters or unimportant matters in your business. Rather, it is about using your time more effectively to manage and prepare for issues before they arise.

To kick-start the process of moving to Quadrant II within our own business, we began writing up basic procedures on how to complete certain tasks within the business.

We have already discussed in a previous chapter the importance of checklists, and we have to admit, the initial checklists that we created related to very simple tasks, such as how to answer the phone and how to clean the dishes.

It might sound like these are such basic activities that they don't require checklists, but implementing systems is a gradual process, and we were careful to start with the easiest tasks so that our staff had the opportunity to become comfortable with the process.

We designed several dot-point checklists that demonstrated how we would like the work to be done within the business, and then we set about hiring (if necessary) and training the team to complete these tasks.

Next, we developed systems to re-educate our clients and customers, as we had created habits with them over the years that we needed to break. Because we were moving away from Quadrant I, we had to encourage our clients to deal with other members of our team. We achieved this by sending out new engagement letters and conducting one-on-one meetings with each client, so we were able to personally introduce them to their new point of contact.

Depending on what stage of the business lifecycle you are in, you may need to spend more time in the other three quadrants before transitioning to Quadrant II. If you're just starting out, for instance, you may need to spend some time in Quadrant III as you get set up. Also, while you are working on systemising your business and implementing an action plan, you will still have to deal with Quadrant I activities as and when they arise.

The fantastic thing about this process is that as you plan, prepare and spend more time in Quadrant II, Quadrant I activities will become few and far between, because you will have anticipated upcoming issues and developed strategies and built strong relationships to help you deal with them.

So just how do you get to Quadrant II? The easiest way is to just say "no".

Sounds simple, doesn't it? This is one of the hardest lessons business owners have to learn when transforming their businesses.

You need to say "no" to things that are not high priorities, but you first need to decide what your priorities are so you can commit to them. Sometimes that is going to mean deciding between two important activities, but you will need to decide what is going to be best for the business.

The hardest area to implement this will be with your clients. You are probably wondering how you can say no to a client or customer, and that's a reasonable concern. Let's take a look at an example within our own accountancy practice.

A client emails Ed a question about land tax because they are thinking about purchasing an investment property. Ed could respond in a number of ways:

Quadrant I: drop everything and respond as soon as the email is received.
Quadrant III: ignore this email and clean out spam email folder
Quadrant IV: forget all about it.
Quadrant II: schedule the request and let the client know exactly when they can expect a response.

In other words, in Quadrant II, Ed has not just said "yes" to the client and made the client's priority his own, but he has planned and prioritised the event.

At Chan & Naylor we have both reduced our working hours by over 80% per week, simply by employing Quadrant II thinking.

Imagine how much calmer your business life would be if you could react like this most of the time.

## TIPS FOR WORKING IN QUADRANT II

Here are some simple things you can do to get working in Quadrant II:

- Set your goals and ensure your vision, goals and plans are all aligned. It will be very difficult to work in Quadrant II if these items are in conflict.

- Turn your goals into specific actions.
- Schedule your entire week with your goals in mind, rather than just taking each day one at a time. This gives you more scope to plan for personal activities such as going to the gym or spending time with family.
- Review your schedule each morning and make any adjustments for unanticipated activities.
- Learn to say “no” to unimportant activities.
- Set priorities and stick to them. If clients are pressuring you for urgent responses, acknowledge their request and schedule a time to respond.
- Be disciplined and stick to your principles and goals, so you can avoid being overwhelmed and forced into a Quadrant I response.
- Remember that you can be efficient with things, but effective with people. People react differently to different situations and you need to be mindful that it is often very difficult to anticipate responses.
- Use your delegation skills to begin the process of transferring Quadrant III and IV activities from your own ’to do’ list.
- Use your delegation skills to transfer important activities
- to your team members and free you up to focus on other planning events. In other words, learn to **let go**.

- Start systemising your business so you can start moving out of Quadrants III and IV and confidently delegate important activities, by training your staff and managing your clients' expectations.

- Understand that from time to time, you will need to work in each of the quadrants but the time spent in inefficient quadrants will reduce as you transform your business.

- Read *The 7 Habits Of Highly Effective People* by Dr Stephen R Covey.

- Read *The E-Myth* by Michael E Gerber.

**PART 10**

# Building Relationships and Trust

Your business has a life of its own and as such, it breeds relationships between a whole range of stakeholders.

Your employees form relationships with each other, with management and with clients. Clients form relationships with your staff and your brand, as do your suppliers. Shareholders and owners form relationships with everyone involved in the business, from staff and management through to clients and suppliers.

All of these different interactions and relationships are vital in order to nurture and build trust and develop culture within your organisation.

We havepreviouslydiscussedthedifferencebetweenefficientand effective people. To be truly effective, you must master interpersonal skills, as they will form the structure of your organisation, create goodwill and add tremendous value to your Balance Sheet.

We all understand the concept of a bank account: if we deposit money into the account we have a credit balance, and if we withdraw money from the account we have less money available to us. If we withdraw even more money from the bank account than we have deposited, we are then in overdraft.

Every human being has an invisible Emotional Bank Account (EBA) with the people they come into contact with throughout their lifetime; it's more commonly known as a relationship. Applying the concept of the EBA in the culture and day-to-day operation of your business is a crucial ingredient in your recipe for success.

Dr Stephen R Covey first coined the phrase Emotional Bank Account in his book *The 7 Habits of Highly Effective People*. The principle behind it is that there is an invisible EBA between people, whether it's between husband and wife, or employer and employee, or between friends. Every organisation has EBAs with their clients/ customers, as well as their staff and suppliers.

When you haven't met someone, generally the EBA is neutral, as you haven't yet formed an opinion or relationship. When you do meet, the EBA is immediately created based on your very first interaction.

Do you remember being young, when your mother told you to shine your shoes and tuck in your shirt so you look the part, and smile and shake hands firmly when you meet someone new, being sure to look them in the eye? This was the first lesson you learnt about creating a good first impression, which allows you to immediately place a deposit into an EBA.

Basically, when one party does something nice for the other person, they invisibly make a deposit into their EBA. Think of EBAs with your personal relationships. When you buy your partner a gift or a bunch of flowers, you are depositing into the EBA, so the account is in credit. When you forget their birthday or let them down, you are withdrawing from the EBA — and if you make too many withdrawals without offering sufficient credits, the bank account could become overdrawn.

Have you ever had a situation arise with a friend or partner where something of a minor nature has triggered a major blow-up, which has taken you by surprise?

Generally the reason behind this is that over a period of time, you were progressively withdrawing from the others person's EBA. You have withdrawn to such an extent that one small incident was the straw that broke the camel's back.

As an example in a business setting, consider this scenario. Maree turns up five minutes late to the weekly staff meeting, and her colleagues and peers are furious. The following week, however, Peter turns up five minutes late to the same meeting — and everyone forgives him.

In Maree's opinion, these two reactions are completely unfair – she believes she should be given the same leeway as Peter. However, what Maree doesn't realise is that in the past, she has withdrawn so much from the EBA with her colleagues by constantly being late, that the account is in the 'red'.

Peter, on the other hand, has always turned up on time and his EBA is in the black. Being late for one meeting constituted a small withdrawal from the EBA, but the account has plenty of credits to cushion it against falling into overdraft.

You have to be mindful that each member of your organisation, and the business itself, has a number of EBAs operating at one time. We spend an enormous amount of time with our staff to ensure that they are paying attention and taking care of all the little tasks for their clients — thus, they're making frequent deposits into their EBA — so that when they make a mistake, the EBA is still in the black and the relationship remains healthy.

Note that we say 'when' they make a mistake, not 'if' they make a mistake, because we are all human, and one day it is likely that we will all make a mistake! This way, the EBA has plenty of credits to ensure that there are 'brownie points' to draw down on if necessary.

| Emotional Bank Account Examples | |
|---|---|
| **Credit/deposits** | Smile when you greet someone for the first time<br>Provide constant feedback<br>Keep open lines of communication<br>Always do what you say you will do<br>Under-promise and over-deliver<br>Be an active listener<br>Always own a problem Be proactive<br>See things from the other person's point of view |
| **Debit/withdrawals** | Over-promise and under-deliver<br>Offer no communication or feedback<br>Do not seek to understand before being<br>understood Be reactive<br>Abdicate not delegate |

The most important relationships in your business are:

1. The relationship between team members

2. The relationship between team members and clients

3. The relationship between managers and technicians

4. The relationship between the organisation and the client

## 1. THE RELATIONSHIP BETWEEN TEAM MEMBERS

Every individual has an EBA with other individuals — and whether the account is in credit or debit depends on how the relationship has developed over the years and the interaction between the individuals.

In any business, staff morale is linked to productivity and if an organisation has low staff morale, it is most likely due to an accumulation of withdrawals from the EBA on the business's behalf. Training staff in the area of interpersonal skills has been a significant factor in the growth of Chan & Naylor, because it provides the team with the skills they need in order to deal with situations with fellow team members, and also with clients and customers.

Whenever there is an issue between team members, we find that it generally surfaces after a minor incident has occurred. This means that a series of withdrawals from the EBA has taken place over a period of time.

We've also found that if the team understands the EBA principle, they can deal with the day-to-day issues with their peers and address and resolve conflicts as and when they occur.

When a new team member joins Chan & Naylor, we emphasise the need to build relationships and deposit into EBAs to build trust. To gain this trust, you must work that little bit extra to start off on the right foot. For example, if you are in a support role and you have to report to a manager, you could ensure that you always provide feedback, and if you're unsure about a task or role, you always ask questions.

Once you have gained trust and deposited into the EBA, other team members will give you autonomy to go about your daily business, trusting that you will get the job done. Yes, we are all human and we all make mistakes, but because you are in so much credit by this stage, if you make an error the withdrawal is not fatal to the relationship — because you have built trust.

## 2. THE RELATIONSHIP BETWEEN TEAM MEMBERS & CLIENTS

Just like your team needs to build relationships and deposit into the EBA with fellow employees to facilitate smooth operations, your staff members also need to develop EBAs with your customers and clients.

Your people are the window to your business, so if your staff are trained on how to answer phones, greet clients, resolve conflict and deal with all other aspects of customer service, then this will create goodwill and deposit into the EBA of your customers.

If the team understands the principles of active listening and conflict resolution, this can assist with depositing into the EBA. The more training you do with your team in this area, the fewer issues you will have to personally handle.

Active listening is the ability to resolve a problem by simply listening to the customer's complaint, and showing empathy and repeating their concerns back to them, generally agreeing with them along the way so as to defuse the situation. It is only once the customer feels that they have been listened to and acknowledged that they will then listen to your perspective and a resolution can be achieved.

Customer service is really all about depositing into the client's EBA. The way that your receptionist and staff members greet the client and the language that they use are all potential deposits. Ask any successful sales person about building relationships with their clients, and they will understand that depositing into the EBA makes them much more effective.

How many times have you walked into a shop and the sales person has ignored you, or they've given you a hard time as if you were simply creating more work for them?

You automatically form a negative opinion of the organisation (a withdrawal from the EBA) based on that interaction. Therefore, training your team so that the point of sale contact creates good first impressions is critical to your business' success.

### THE CLIENT'S POINT OF VIEW

Every industry evolves its own language and terminology to explain technical information or concepts. Unfortunately, every industry also falls into the trap of assuming that everyone they speak to understands their jargon.

This is particularly true of the professional services industry, including accountants, lawyers, architects, doctors, engineers and computer technicians. Far too often we hear complaints from clients that our technical people talk 'shop' and use language that they don't understand. Most technical areas are complicated enough and sometimes we forget that our clients do not understand the terms we use in our day-to-day work.

Depending on the type of business that you run, you need to be aware that most of your clients do not understand your lingo. At Chan & Naylor, for example, our clients come from different education and working backgrounds and may simply not have been exposed to many of the terms that we use. Dividends, CGT, FBT, capitalising, rebates... these are just a few of the terms that we take for granted in our business. For some of our clients, we may as well be speaking Swahili when we explain their accounts to them!

At Chan & Naylor we realise that good client service doesn't just mean getting the job done on time, but also helping the client understand. When we become conscious of using too much jargon, we need to make an effort and change the way we use our terms.

The most important thing we have realised is that clients will not tell you that they do not understand you — they will simply leave rather than feel stupid in front of you.

This realisation helped us to decide that it is important for us to educate our staff, so we have created a set of terms that have become part of our culture.

We regularly hold team-training sessions to remind our staff members of these terms and reinforce the importance of avoiding jargon when talking to clients. We have created checklists of the most commonly used terms, and how to answer these in layman's terms.

For example, instead of using the terms 'debtors' and 'creditors', we talk to the client about 'people that owe you money' and 'people you owe money to'. Every industry will have its own technical jargon.

We have found that improving the interpersonal skills of our team has had enormous benefits for our firm. You can also achieve these benefits with a regular training program that helps generate deposits into your client's EBAs.

It is vital to make sure your team understands that it is not necessarily how proficient they are with technical skills that will make them successful in their chosen field — it's good social and interpersonal skills that will ultimately make or break their career. The most successful accountants in our organisation are not necessarily the most technically proficient, but they are the ones who form good relationships with their clients.

As with many things, the 80/20 rule applies in this situation – 80% of your time is spent on the technical aspect of a job, and 20% of your time is spent liaising and discussing issues with clients/customers. More importantly, it is that 20% that gives your firm 80% of the overall result.

That is to say that how you explain things to your client, how you talk to them and how well you relate to them as people play a vital role in the relationship. Taking a personal interest, such as, "Hi Brett, how are the kids and family?" or "Hi Joan, happy birthday for yesterday", is precisely the type of interaction that creates 80% of the overall result and goodwill. If it becomes entrenched in your culture, you will have delighted clients referring a constant stream of business to your company.

Just remember that the more work and training you put into the interpersonal skills and culture of your team, the more leverage you can achieve with your time, and the more the business starts to work without you.

## 3. THE RELATIONSHIP BETWEEN MANAGERS & TECHNICIANS

Every business is made up of different levels of management and team members. A manager is the leader in his or her own right, but in order to be effective — and to get maximum results — the manager needs the support of his or her team and vice-versa.

It is critical that the team is working together and communicating, just like members of a successful football team communicate on the playing field to let each other know what is happening. This builds trust and cohesion among the people working alongside you and shows that as a manager, you are the captain of this team.

Whenever a new staff member is inducted into our organisation, we emphasise that the most important thing they need to work on in the early days of building working relationships is opening the communication lines with the staff around them, by providing constant feedback either up or down the chain.

The manager must build trust and relationships with the people working directly beneath them, and the technician must do the same with the manager. Communication and feedback generates deposits into the EBA of both parties, and down the track when a mistake occurs, it isn't fatal to the relationship.

You can create systems to ensure that good communication practices occur between team members, via regular activities such as weekly staff meetings, team outings, staff training on interpersonal skills and so on.

Of course, sometimes some relationships do not always work, and some personalities turn out to be the genuinely wrong fit for your business. That is why we place such importance on regular performance reviews, which enable us to discuss these issues and deal with them swiftly to ensure high staff morale.

The only way you can leverage your time and effort is through systems and your people, so it's vital that your managers are able to get the best from their team.

## 4. THE RELATIONSHIP BETWEEN THE ORGANISATION & THE CLIENT

Your business and your client have an EBA, which is developed in the way that the business communicates and markets itself. The use of language in newsletters and correspondence, the way that your business presents itself, how your people dress and relate to the client — these are all opportunities to make deposits into or withdrawals from the EBA.

Remember that a disgruntled client is more likely to tell other potential clients if they have had a bad experience with your organisation, so it's critical that you take every opportunity to foster relationships and generate deposits into your business's EBA. The best way to achieve this is via your people, your product and your service.

Your organisation can systemise many parts of the business to help generate EBA deposits. Here are some simple systems that we have adopted that have worked well for Chan & Naylor:

### *1. TELEPHONE SCRIPTS*

To create good first impressions, everyone in our office — from the receptionist right through to the partners and CEO — answers the telephone in exactly the same manner.

Our standard greeting is: "Good morning/afternoon, welcome to Chan & Naylor, this is [Name]."

Studies have shown that this is a very effective way of answering the telephone, because by using the word "welcome" you are creating a warm feeling with the client.

Also, by placing the words "this is" in front of the person's name, you provide time for the caller to hear and understand the name of the person who has answered the phone.

### *2. UNIFORMS*

We introduced uniforms into our organisation as part of the systemisation process. We were one of the first accounting firms to introduce uniforms and many of our peers scoffed at the move, saying that they couldn't see the point to it, and predicted that it would be impossible to have our team conform.

It was a challenge to get everyone on the team on board, we must admit. But once we educated them about why we wanted to introduce uniforms, and set up a team to co-ordinate the design, we had the support of every member of staff. It was challenging in the beginning, yes, but persistence paid off and now our uniform is an important part of our culture.

By creating a corporate culture and uniformity, we indirectly build trust with our clients and our team (EBA), as the client is reassured that they are dealing with an organisation rather than individuals.

Many accountants in the industry feel that it is impossible to leverage their own service because the client wants to deal with them personally. However, we have found that clients are happy to deal with anyone within our team, provided that there is consistency in the delivery of the service.

Clients and customers do not like change, so we realised it was important to maintain consistency — and a very simply way to achieve this was in the way that we look. Now, whether the client sees the partner or a manager, if their experience is 80% the same each time, they won't leave. That is why franchises are so successful!

### 3. CHECKLISTS/PROCESSES

To ensure consistency in the delivery of our services, we introduced checklists on every service that our organisation offers. This ensures that not only do all of our staff members look similar (due to uniforms), but they also each deliver the same service via the use of checklists and procedures.

This serves to minimise errors and when these checklists were introduced, it leveraged our skills and our time, so we could spent our time developing other parts of Chan & Naylor. Most importantly, it created trust, and now our client's experience — whether they meet with us, a partner or another team member — is 80% the same.

### 4. WEBSITE/BROCHURE

A website and brochure is an essential marketing tool for your organisation and helps build relationships with your clients. If you don't have the resources to develop a website in-house, we would strongly recommend that you invest the time and money to have a professional design and produce it on your behalf. The additional revenue you generate from this marketing tool will more than recover the cost of developing a professional website, so consider it an investment in your Balance Sheet.

Testimonials from clients are another essential component of your marketing. Ask your best clients for a referral and place it prominentlyinthebrochureoronyourwebsite. It helps todemonstrate credibility and adds a genuinely human aspect to the business.

The information that you include on your website and in brochures should outline all of the products and/or services you provide. Presentation is everything and your website and marketing brochures must be consistent with your brand.

### *TEAM RECOGNITION — STAR AWARD SYSTEM*

An incentive or bonus system will encourage your team members to work together to meet budgets and successfully achieve other tasks.

A system that worked for us in our growth phase was a Star Award program, which was brought to our attention through one of our clients who worked for a major bank in human resources.

The bank had just taken over another institution and they were experiencing issues with team morale during the transition. The bank contracted a large US human resource consultant to provide solutions, which subsequently selected the Star Award system. We borrowed the idea and successfully adopted it in our organisation, and it worked like a charm.

The point of the system is to encourage our team members to acknowledge kind deeds towards each other and allow clients to give positive feedback. Whenever someone performs an act beyond the call of duty (it cannot simply be doing their normal job), they can be nominated for a Star Award.

The criteria for nominating someone for a Star Award are as follows:

- Extra help given to meet deadlines, or dropping whatever you are doing to help.
- Special mention from a client on a survey.
- Client goes out of their way to call and say that you did a good job.
- 3 Stars = $50 gift voucher.

The Star Award year runs parallel to the financial year, from 1 July to 30 June. On 1 July each year, each staff member's overall Star Awards tally goes back to nil, but any outstanding stars are carried forward to be included in the next gift voucher count.

The procedure for nominating someone for a Star Award is as follows:

- You need to fill out a nomination form, which will be kept with the committee.
- Once you have filled out the nomination form, you must give it to the manager in charge for approval.
- On the wall next to the yearly planner is a register, which will indicate where employees currently stand with their nominations.
- Each week the committee goes through award nominations to tally up who gets nominated.
- Every nomination that has been approved will be recorded on the register and stars put up on the board.
- An email is sent to all staff members, summarising the awards for the week.
- For every three stars earned, each nominated employee will receive a $50 gift voucher. The reward is marked with a highlighter on the board.
- Gift vouchers are handed out every week at the staff training meeting.

- At the end of each financial year, all of the nomination forms are collected and tallied, and the overall results are provided to the partners for management assessment.

This program encourages teamwork, provides incentives for completing day-to-day tasks and creates a fun atmosphere. It also rewards good performers.

> **Helpful Hint: Present the Star Awards gift vouchers at staff meetings so that your entire team acknowledges the recipient. This creates a great atmosphere and fun environment. Also, when a Star Award nomination has been received, send an email to all staff explaining who has been nominated and why.**

## FINAL THOUGHTS

Before we move on from this topic, we thought it was worthwhile mentioning a couple of key philosophies that have helped shape our culture at Chan & Naylor.

Understanding the other person's point of view may sound simple enough, but if everyone did this in practice, we would all have overflowing EBAs! Dr Steven Covey described this as "seek to understand, before being understood".

There is a phrase, "No one has a finer command of the English language than the person who keeps his mouth shut!"

When you have a point to make, you should always allow the other person to 'download' their frustrations first, so you can seek to understand things from their point of view before you respond. This means listening to what they have to say and being empathetic and caring about their complaint.

It is only once they feel that they have been understood that they will lower their guard to listen to what you have to say.

Most people handle complaints by trying to get the other person to understand their point of view first, without listening to them. Both sides are debating their side of the story, but no one is really listening. This creates an argument where both parties try to shout the other person down and no one feels that they, or their complaints, have been truly understood or listened to.

If you seek to understand the other person's position first, and you genuinely attempt to see things from their point of view, you will be making a deposit into that person's EBA. With some credit in their EBA, they will be more likely to listen to you and extend you the same courtesy.

We train our staff to role-play these types of situations so that they are caring and empathetic towards our clients' concerns.

Another of our key philosophies is simple, but very effective: under-promise and over-deliver. Unfortunately, many people and businesses over-promise and under-deliver. You may have even done this yourself unintentionally, when you tell someone you will get back to them by Monday, but you don't get a chance to do it until Thursday.

At Chan & Naylor, our staff are trained to under-promise and over-deliver in all situations. This means that if they say they will deliver a document to you on Tuesday then, come rain, hail or shine, they will deliver it to you on Tuesday. They are trained not to make a promise they cannot deliver. In fact, they have even been trained to say it will be ready on Thursday, and then deliver it the day before, on Wednesday.

It's all about managing and meeting expectations and, where possible, exceeding them. It's also about building your reputation by delivering on your promises. The most important point to remember is that it's always best to say nothing at all, rather than make a promise that you cannot deliver.

**PART 11**

# The Power of Leverage

The word 'leverage' means 'to gain a strategic advantage'. In financial terms, when you're investing with borrowed money, it is a way to amplify your potential gains by using someone else's (the bank's) money.

In other words, it is the power to act effectively. Leverage is all about using the tools and resources around you to improve your position, and make 1 + 1 = 3.

In order for your business to be successful, you must understand the concept of leverage and how it applies practically in the day-to-day running of your business.

As we have mentioned earlier in this book, an important part of creating and growing a successful business lies in understanding that you may need to change your mindset. The skills you require to do the job are not the same skills you need to get someone *else* to do the job — and that's the real secret to passive income. You may need to re-educate and re-program yourself to become a manager, and you can do this by reading and attending seminars, for example, which is a valuable re-investment.

The most successful entrepreneurs in the world understand that they need to surround themselves with people who can assist them in the areas that they are weak in. Therefore, it's important that you know your strengths and weaknesses, so you can leverage your weaknesses to turn them into strengths by harnessing the knowledge of others in your team.

## LEVERAGE YOUR PEOPLE

As a small business owner aiming to grow your profits, time management is one of the most crucial areas that you will need to master. In order to free up your own time so you can work on "Important, but Not Urgent" (Quadrant II) activities, you will need to leverage your time through your team and the development of systems and training.

This is a very important part of growing your business, because by freeing up your time to work in these areas and getting out of the day-to-day operations, you can start duplicating the processes that generate your business income.

For instance, let's assume that you are personally doing the work and in doing so, you generate $50,000 in profits per year. One day you decide to employ somebody, train them and have them produce the same work that you were producing. To make it worth your while, they would need to produce $50,000 in profits — over and above expenses, such as their wages.

This means that you might need the employee to generate turnover of $100,000, in order to cover their wages and other expenses, which we'll estimate at $50,000.

With a turnover of $100,000 and expenses of $50,000, you're left with a profit of $50,000 — and you don't have to physically do the work yourself.

Now, let's imagine that you could duplicate this process with another nine people. You would then have 10 staff members working for you, generating $500,000 in profit per year. In doing this you have effectively leveraged your time, as you're now free to work in the right areas of your business.

Instead of doing all the technical work of your business, plus the marketing and PR, management and training, you can now simplify and streamline your workload so that you're just concentrating on developing marketing and sales leads. Someone else is carrying out the technical work — in fact, many other people are doing it — which allows you to concentrate on strategies to generate more sales.

Of course, in order to effectively leverage your staff, you need to foster a happy working environment so staff morale is high and your employees are actively engaged. That's why it's so important that you meet the needs of your team.

No matter what industry you're in or how many staff you employ, each member of your team essentially has four needs:

1. **To be appreciated.** Show your appreciation via programs such as employee recognition awards, and/or a bonus system. Work towards an Employee of the Year award, which is collected from the votes of

their peers. Create a staff review process twice a year to discuss their performance and their short and long-term goals.

2. **To be challenged at work.** Ensure that senior people are not doing mundane work that is below their skill level — not only will they become bored, but also it's an inefficient use of resources. Instead, introduce junior or less qualified staff who can assist and support the more senior staff.

Teach your managers to delegate work and manage their own workflow. Keep encouraging them to delegate and manage only.
It is absolutely imperative that you create this kind of leveraging throughout your business, because tremendous profits can be achieved. It is simply about getting less qualified or junior people to do the work, which is processed through your systems into extraordinary results. All of this results in greater profits and happier team members who will not burn out.

1. **To be well remunerated.** Ensure that your employees are paid well above award wages by managing the business well. This can only be the case if there is a win for the client, a win for the employee and a win for the owner, all at the same time. Good management on the owner's part can achieve this.

   Make sure that you run the business with the right staff, the right systems in place and the right clients. With the juniors or less qualified staff doing the lower-end work, everybody wins: clients win because you're producing the service or product as economically as possible, and your staff members win because they are gaining relevant, practical experience that will help them to move forward in their career.

2. **To achieve balance.** Ideally and dependant on your industry, your senior managers should be able to produce three times their salary in the hours between 9am and 5pm. If this is not being achieved, then perhaps you need to look at a few things:

- Are they doing too much low-level work? If so, they may not be delegating effectively; the staff below them may not be competent; or they may not be utilising their resources correctly.

- Do they lack the management, delegation and training skills? If so, arrange the appropriate training so they can acquire the skills they need.

- Are they incompetent? If so consider whether they are suitable for the role and whether their future lies with your business.

## LEVERAGE YOUR EQUITY & CASH FLOW

In the coming chapters we are going to talk more about using your cash flow and the profits of your business to invest and build wealth.

Did you know that if your business generates sustainable profits, and has assets and goodwill, it might be possible to borrow against all of this and access a loan from the bank? It is very similar to borrowing against the security of a property, except that you're putting your business up as security.

Many franchises, long-standing businesses and professional services industries are viewed as being reasonable security risks by banks. By tapping into this equity and using it to invest in other asset classes, you gain access to substantial leverage opportunities that can help you to fast track your wealth.

This may not be available to all businesses and the amount that the bank will lend you against the assets of your business may be lower than that which is available with property, but at the very least if you have a trading history, an unsecured overdraft will provide you with some leverage to help with cash flow.

## LEVERAGE YOUR PROFITS

If we were to tell you that you could increase your profits by up to 400%, without spending any more time in your business, you might think we've lost the plot!

But bear with us for a moment, and let us show you the principle that we successfully applied at Chan & Naylor, as this principle can be applied in almost every business:

20% Customers
= produce
**80% Profit**

80% Customers
= produce
**20% Profit**

Essentially what this means is that 20% of your customers produce 80% of your profits, and the remaining 80% of your customers produce just 20% of your profits.

Hence, to increase profits you simply need to focus more attention on customers that generate 80% of your business' profits. You can then delegate the work of the 80% of customers that produce only 20% of the profits to other team members, as this provides you with a further 80% of your own time/capacity to work with the more profitable clients.

| | |
|---|---|
| 20% Customers x 5 | = 100% of your customers and 100% of your time and energy = produce |
| **80% Profit** | **x 5 = 400% of your income** |

In the above example, you are multiplying the amount of good quality, profitable clients that you work with — which allows you to boost your profits by 400%, without having to spend any extra time in the business.

So just how did we practically achieve this at Chan & Naylor?

It was all about identifying where our time was best spent in the business. In the early days, we achieved this by delegating the "factory work" on 80% of clients — those ones that only generated 20% of our profits — to our staff.

We developed systems and undertook training to ensure quality control and maintenance of service levels. We also educated our clients and encouraged them to work with our staff, by explaining that they were far better off having a team of people available to service them, rather than just one of us as an individual.

We were able to focus more of our time on product and service development, which helped all of our clients, and we spent more personalised time on the 20% of our client base that generated 80% of our profits.

Yes, we lost some clients due to this change and we were prepared to accept this. The clients that did stay with us under the new system benefited in the long run, because we both had more time to spend on strategic areas within the business. This in turn created efficiencies, products, services and wealth creation strategies that helped to increase our clients' wealth.

This model meant that our profits soared, without us having to spend any more time in the business. As the business grew, over time, we were able to replace ourselves by hiring more senior people. We also established Joint Venture Partners who took on this role, which then enabled us to step out of the business altogether.

## LEVERAGE YOUR BRAND

To most of you, this concept may be a little way down the track, but at least if you start with the end goal in mind, you can begin to see what is really achievable.

Chan & Naylor has spent two decades building a brand, both within the accounting industry among its peers, and in the professional services area in relation to offering wealth-creation structuring via property and taxation services to its clients.

This has not happened by accident. In fact, it has taken considerable time, effort and money to achieve this. However, we view the investment in the brand as a Balance Sheet item that helps to build long-term wealth.

Many people buy into franchises because of the power of the brand, such as McDonald's and KFC. The brand is essentially a combination of all things we have discussed in this book: the systems, the people, the product or service, the marketing and the intellectual property.

Over time, if you invest in your brand, you will have the ability to leverage this. Chan & Naylor is now a well-known brand in the financial services, wealth creation, property investment structuring, small business and taxation space.

We have a reputation for being the number one accountants in the country to work with if you invest in property, and we have established joint ventures with other like-minded business owners across Australia (similar to a franchise deal).

Our joint venture partner's can leverage off the Chan & Naylor brand, which adds to their Balance Sheets, creating a win/ win situation for all parties. We explain this in more detail shortly.

One of the most important lessons you will learn throughout your journey is that you cannot grow your business all by yourself; you will need the help of many people and many other organisations along the way.

We learnt this lesson very early on and it was a clear strategy on our part to form strategic alliances with organisations and people whose services are complementary to what we do. There always has to be a win/win outcome in this form of a relationship for it to work.

To provide you with an example, over the years we have had very successful relationships with different organisations in the property arena, including buyer's agents and financiers. Their aim is to assist clients in sourcing the right type of property for the right price, and finance the property. As accountants, our aim is to assist people in structuring their assets correctly from a taxation, estate planning and asset protection point of view, and help them manage their yearly compliance work.

Our various businesses have different purposes, but in combination, our alliance works well. We have even pooled our resources on occasion to hold seminars together, which serves to attract people who are interested in both services.

We have made and continue to make alliance partnerships over the years that benefit both parties, and we are always mindful that there must be a win/ win outcome for it to succeed.

## LEVERAGE VIA JOINT VENTURES AND PARTNERSHIPS

We have always gone into business relationships with a win/ win mindset, because time and time again we have seen relationships fail due to the establishment of lose/win scenarios.

Put simply, the deal has to be fair and equitable to all parties involved. As our business became more successful we realised that in order to expand the

Chan & Naylor brand nationally, we had to form win/win relationships with likeminded, passionate, "Abundant" type people across the country.

We decided upon a joint venture partnership (JVP) model, which is a sustainable model that provides each partner with up to 50% equity in the business. As a result, both partners have a vested interest in ensuring growth and sustainability.

This is unlike the traditional franchise model, where the franchisor has little interest in the franchisee's bottom line. Instead, you find that the traditional franchisor is more focused on establishing new franchisees, because earning royalties from new franchisees is where they derive the most of their income.

The Chan & Naylor JV model is quite different because head office is a shareholder in the joint venture partnership, and hence we have an interest in the net profit that the enterprise generates. We're extremely interested in helping our JVP's become as profitable as they possibly can, which, once again, creates a win/win scenario for everyone.

This type of equity JV model ensures that both Chan & Naylor and our JVP's work in partnership and understand each other's roles. Each partner recognises their own strengths and weaknesses, and we leverage off each other's strengths to achieve a win/win.

For example, Chan & Naylor's role is that of a strategic nature, including aspects such as managing the marketing, brand, public relations, system development, product development, strategic alliance relationships and strategic direction. Meanwhile, the local JVP is responsible for and empowered to manage the local operation, including the staff and the clients, to ensure a profitable result.

Ultimately, the success or failure of a JVP, as with any franchise, is determined by the people who are involved and their ability to understand the win/win philosophy. They need to have an "Abundant" mindset, and they also need to have the ability to work within a system.

Although Chan & Naylor is ranked 40th in the top 100 BRW Firms around Australia and has become a national firm with offices in nearly every state, each local office offers a high level of customer service and the attention to detail that you might expect of a smaller firm. Essentially, it's the best of both worlds: the backing and resources of a national company, but the personalised level of service of an owner-operated business where the people you work with are the people who actually co-own the business.

The biggest beneficiary of this model are the clients, because at a local office they are dealing with co-owners of the business, who have a genuine vested interest to ensure that excellent service levels to clients are maintained.

We've learnt over the years that in order for these JVP's to be successful, it is crucial that all parties in the joint venture understand each other's functions and responsibilities. That way, everyone is aligned and on the same page as they work toward the same successful outcome. To achieve this, we make sure we invest in forming a good working relationship, as open lines of communication are essential for success in any field.

# PART 12

# Your Business and investing

In this chapter and the next, we'll explore the principles of leveraging your business success in order to accelerate your personal wealth.

We'll also discuss business structures, which is an area of business development that many people fail to give proper attention to.

## ADOPTING A LONG TERM VIEW

For those of you just starting out in business, or those who are facing the day-to-day challenges of simply keeping your business afloat, the idea of generating your personal wealth may seem a long way off — or out of reach completely.

However, it's important that you learn and understand these principles early on. If you can begin to appreciate what can be achieved once your business becomes a finely tuned machine — one that provides you with regular, sustainable cash flow and profits without you necessarily working in the business — you can start to see how you can use these strategies to accelerate your own personal net worth.

We often ask business owners why they have taken the risk to set up and operate their own business. A common response is, "To create a passive income whereby the business takes care of itself and to provide for the family."

Yes, we often hear that they want to be their own boss and cast off the shackles of the '9 to 5 grind', but given the risk and enormous effort involved in running a business, their true motivation usually runs deeper than that. It's usually a desire to create a flexible, supportive financial structure that will look after them and their family well into retirement.

Business owners work harder and smarter than most regular employees as there is no luxury of sitting on the sidelines — ever. Particularly in the early days, it's up to them to source the business and generate an income. It is therefore even more crucial that you learn strategies to leverage your time, assets and creativity.

The question then becomes: "How can I leverage my business to improve my personal wealth situation?"

It is seldom as simple as growing the business and ignoring other assets, as the lines can be blurred or can even complement each other. For example, you might consider how you may be able to use your super fund contributions to help grow a property portfolio, while at the same time improve your business.

One answer could be to purchase the Business real property that you operate your business using your Self Managed Super Fund, so you can then borrow against the asset, using your superannuation contributions and rent to pay for the property.

Many clients come to us and complain that their current advisers say this is not possible, but we've found that in many cases, it is possible: all they needed was the right advice from suitably qualified accountants, lawyers and financial planners.

The problem is, not all advisers think the same, and they can have competing objectives and agendas. At Chan & Naylor, we take a more holistic approach to wealth creation, and we work with clients to help them find the best advisers who will complement each other so as to achieve the best outcomes for our clients.

## THE FOUR-PHASE LIFE CYCLE

We see a lot of people travelling through the following four phases in their life — we liken it to the four quarters of a sports match:

- First Quarter — up to age 20: education phase
- Second Quarter — age 21–40: family set-up phase
- Third Quarter — age 41–60: accumulation phase
- Fourth Quarter — age 60+, last part of life: retirement phase

All too often, people wait until they're in their 50's before they start to acquire wealth. By this stage, they have paid down the family home, paid for their kids' education and they've bought some comfort items, and whatever is leftover is put towards their own wealth creation.

If your life were a World Series sports match, would you wait until the third or fourth quarter to pile on the scoreboard? It could be too late, and you may not have left yourself enough time to really enjoy the fruits of your labour. If you start as early as possible, however, and begin moving towards your own wealth position as a standard course — rather than simply using whatever is leftover — you could find yourself in a different situation entirely.

Both Ed and David have been successful in building businesses, however, this is only part of their success. It is what they have done with the profits generated from their business that has truly created their personal wealth.

For instance, Ed and David are passionate property investors. They have each built significant real estate portfolios, which they simply view and treat as another business. For more detailed stories and information behind how they fast-tracked their wealth through property investing, I would recommend that you read *How To Legally Reduce Your Tax* and *Creating Wealth For Life Through Property Investment.*

However, in this chapter we'll move on to discuss how you, as the owner of a business, can use the principles of leverage to parlay your business achievements into a wider wealth-creation model — allowing you to reap personal profits, as well as business success.

Essentially, there are five basic strategies to follow that will make all the difference between a successful wealth-creation plan, and one that flounders.

### 1. INTELLIGENT USE OF DEBT

Most of us have had it ingrained that 'debt is the devil'. We work endless hours to pay off our home mortgages, so the idea of going into more debt for our business can seem overwhelming. But the truth is, when you leverage debt correctly, it is your friend, not your enemy. Of course, it's important to have financial buffers in place so that you're adequately prepared to manage your debts without feeling pressured.

### 2. SELECT THE RIGHT ASSET CLASS

You need an asset class that allows you to maximise leverage. For Ed and David, this was property. For you and your situation, it may be shares or managed funds. You can choose any asset class you like, but one important point to keep in mind is that you must learn about it until you know it inside out. Focus creates experience, which creates success, which creates confidence — so make sure you are committed to the process.

### 3. BUY TIME

Time will create gains and reduce risk. When you invest in property, a piece of art or shares, most people believe it is the actual asset that they are investing in. While this is obviously true, the real thing you're investing in is time. You're banking on the fact that, by holding on to that asset for a certain period of time, it will increase in value. So ask yourself: how long will it take for that asset to grow in value, and can I afford to hold it long enough to realise that gain?

### 4. USE THE RIGHT STRUCTURE

It's important to structure your assets correctly so that they are protected against risks, such as being sued. The right structure and estate-planning model can provide flexibility and protection, and reduce your exposure to risks.

### 5. LEVERAGE

It's been covered many times already in this book, but it really is vital that you surround yourself with — and leverage off — knowledgeable people including bankers, financial advisers and agents. If you are the smartest person on your team, you are in trouble.

Underpinning these five basic principles is your mindset. Wealthier people think differently to others, as they are committed to expanding their knowledge, mixing with like-minded people and, above all, they have a determined desire to succeed. They will use all the tools available to them to ensure success, and their mindset is set to a level that acknowledges and accepts opportunities that come their way.

As an analogy, think of your mindset as if it is a bucket. Wealthy people have big buckets, so they can capture more of everything: ideas, opportunities, prospects and growth. The first stage of wealth creation is to train your mind to become a bigger bucket. For most people, fear stops them from taking the steps they need to take to become successful. Fear of debt, fear of failure and yes, even fear of success.

Taking all of the above into account, it's clear that through the use of leverage and intelligent debt (with appropriate buffers), you can build your asset base in a way that suits your business and your risk profile. The higher your asset base, the greater your wealth potential.

If your mindset is the size of your bucket, and your wealth is how you fill it, then to maximise your efforts you must also focus on possible leaks, as leaks reduce your wealth. Think of structures, estate planning, leverage and buying time as strategies you can use to reduce the possibility of leaks. These strategies are akin to plugging possible holes in your wealth bucket.

### *5. LEVERAGING DEBT*

Wealth is the growth of your net assets, which is the value of your assets less any debts/liabilities.

What maximises the growth is the increasing value of your assets, as the debt stays stable. As a basic example, if you borrow

$100 to buy an asset, you owe $100, but the asset that you buy with that money may grow in value to $200. The growth in the asset value does not increase your debt.

Let's look at this more closely, with an example of five investors using different levels of debt to invest in an asset:

### *POOR THINKING V'S RICH THINKING*

### *THE POWER OF DEBT/LEVERAGE*

Growth/Yield 10% + 4% = 14% total

Interest Rate (7%)

Net Return 7%

| Cash | **Inv 1**<br>$100k | **Inv 2**<br>$100k | **Inv 3**<br>$100k | **Inv 4**<br>$100k | **Inv 5**<br>$0 |
|---|---|---|---|---|---|
| Debt amount | $(0) | $(100)K | $(400)K | $(900) K | $(1000) |
| Investment | $100K | $200K | $500K | $1000K | $1000 |
| Net Return | $14K | $21K | $42K | $77K | $70K |
| **Cash Return** | 14% | 21% | 42% | 77% | Infinity |
| **Debt %** | 0% | 50% | 80% | 90% | 100% |

Conclusion: Higher Debt = Higher Return

As you can see, Investor 3 borrowed 80% of the asset value, and they received a 42% return on their money. Many of us have experienced this with our own home, as growth happens regularly with every property cycle, on average every seven to 10 years.

So how can we apply the same outcome to other investments? We borrow to buy the family home because our fear of not having a roof over our heads is greater than the fear of the debt. Most people then pay the debt down as quickly as possible.

But what if you did things differently? What if, instead of paying the mortgage as quickly as possible, you maintained this level of debt and redirected the funds that would have gone towards the mortgage to purchase a second property?

There's normally no impact on the amount of money coming out of your pocket each month but, by redistributing where the money goes, you now have two properties. Certainly there is more risk involved when you increase your debt levels, but over time this creates more wealth. The following table demonstrates how this could work:

| **Homeowner 1: Jenny**<br>Principal & Interest Loan, Own Home | **Homeowner 2: Richard**<br>Interest-Only Loan, Own Home | **Homeowner 2: Richard**<br>Interest-Only Loan, Investment Property | **Options** |
|---|---|---|---|
| **Year 1**<br>Market Value $500,000<br>Debt $500,000<br>Equity nil | **Year 1**<br>Market Value $500,000<br>Debt $500,000<br>Equity nil | **Year 1**<br>Market Value $500,000<br>Debt $500,000<br>Equity nil | |
| **Year 10**<br>Market Value $1m Debt $350,000 Equity $650,000 | **Year 10**<br>Market Value $1m Debt $500,000 Equity $500,000 | **Year 10**<br>Market Value $1m Debt $500,000 Equity $500,000 | Sell investment property and pay off home loan. No more debt and you own your home outright, worth $1m. Less CGT. |
| **Year 20**<br>Market Value $2m Debt $165,000 Equity $1.85m | **Year 20**<br>Market Value $2m Debt $500,000 Equity $1.5m | **Year 20**<br>Market Value $2m Debt $500,000 Equity $1.5m | Perhaps Homeowner 1 moves to an interest only loan and contribute funds into super.As super is taxed at 15%, compared to up to 47% in your hands, there is a potential 32% saving. She could then use her super funds upon retirement to pay out her home loan. |
| **Year 30**<br>Market Value $4m Debt $0<br>Equity $4m | **Year 30**<br>Market Value $4m Debt $500,000 Equity $3.5m | **Year 30**<br>Market Value $4m Debt $500,000 Equity $3.5m | |
| | Combined equity = $7m Subtract Additional Interest $320,000 on home loan. Subtract Rent Shortfall $450,000 | | |
| Total equity $4m | Total equity = $6.23m | | |

Note: Licenced Financial Planner Advice Required

## SUMMARY

1. If you pay off your home in 30 years, your equity (net assets) would be $4 million at year 30.

2. If you pay only interest on your home loan and use the additional funds to pay the shortfall in a second property, after 30 years you would have $6.23 million in equity (net assets) — a $2.23 million improvement.

**Note:** figures may differ depending on interest rates and marginal tax rates used

## CASH FLOW

When we invest in property assets, we look for high capital growth properties in good locations with strong track records over many decades. The only downside with this type of investment is that it's generally negatively geared, meaning the income received is less than what it costs you to hold it — thereby creating a loss. This loss is tax deductible and is often referred to as 'negative gearing'.

There are many tax considerations to take into account when planning your investments. For instance, if you invest in a negatively geared property, it doesn't make much sense to buy in a company name, as you will pay tax at the corporate rate of 30% on any capital gains — and you'll have no access to the Capital Gains Tax 50% discount if and when you sell.

It makes more sense to receive 100% of the cash flow before any tax is sent off to the tax office. The following diagram illustrates this point in more detail and shows how you can secure an investment property in a trust and get:

1. The maximum available asset protection;

2. Profits that can be distributed to the lowest taxpayer, as the trust secures the property and pays down the interest expense; and

3. Much-improved estate planning.

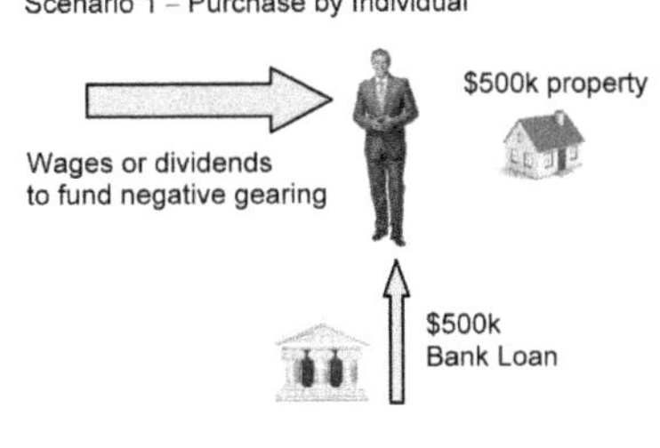


Scenario 1

- Individual owns property and borrows personally
    - No asset protection
    - Limited estate planning
    - No flexibility
    - All income and capital gains at individual's marginal tax rate
- Timing difference when individual receives tax benefit of negative gearing (can apply for tax variation). Similar timing difference whether individual receives wage or dividends to fund negative gearing. More administration
- Does not allow for major changes to individual's circumstances

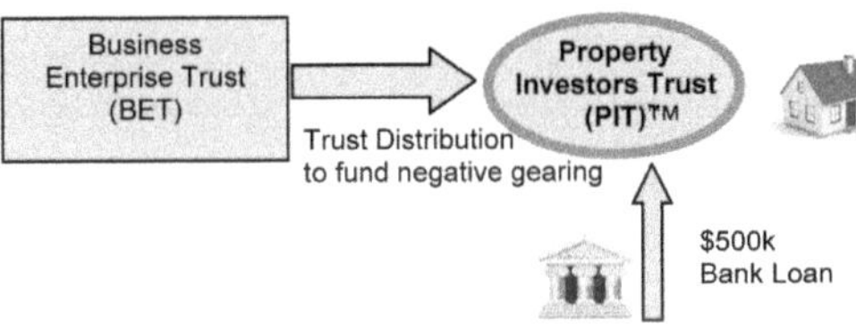


Scenario 2

- PIT™ owns property and borrows
    - Asset protection
    - Improved estate planning
    - Flexible
    - All income and capital gains is made by the trust and so can be distributed to anyone
- Negative gearing funded by a trust distribution from the BET after ticking Family Trust Election. This distribution reduces what would be available to distribute to others. Therefore, no difference to current negative gearing whether property purchased in business owner's name or PIT,™ but significant differences long term
- Ownership within the trust allows for major changes to individual's circumstances without needing to transfer property to different owner, which would trigger CGT and stamp

In this example, Scenario 2 allows you to distribute profits from your business into your assets tax effectively, because it uses pre-tax profits from your business to fund the negative gearing of the property purchased in the Property Investor Trust™. You can also readily manage your cash flow and easily separate your personal wealth creation from your business.

Scenario 1 shows what the typical PAYG person would need to do to achieve a similar but much less effective outcome.

Of course, these examples relate to complex financial and taxation decisions, and you should always seek appropriate professional advice according to your own personal circumstances before making any big financial decisions. But as this diagram illustrates, there are many options available to you, and making the right decisions early on in your business life cycle can pay dividends for many years to come.

PART 13

# Your Business Structure

This is an area that is often neglected by the owners of many businesses, but it can have a significant impact on your net worth if you get this wrong upfront.

When entrepreneurs start a business, their thoughts are often on cash flow, market positioning, financing, employees, work hours, risk and the like. They seldom look at what is the best business ownership structure to achieve these outcomes and longer term wealth creation. Even fewer think of the cycles their business will travel through or the changes that are going to occur over time, both to the business and to themselves and their family.

When launching a business, you should always consider what structure is best suited to your business, now and in the future, and the reasons why. Business structure is something you need to address before you start opening bank accounts, signing leases, purchasing plant and equipment, employing staff and registering any intellectual property. It should be step one.

At Chan & Naylor, we believe that you should always start with the end in mind. This means that when you're launching your business, you need to give due consideration to your long-term goals and needs. For instance, you may one day wish to protect the assets that you have built, you may require flexibility if your circumstances change, you might want to sell part of your business, or you may want to bring in new partners.

The structure that you use to set up your business will impact your abilities to make these decisions in the future. It is an area that is often neglected by business owners, and unfortunately this neglect can cost them tens of thousands of dollars or indeed much more if they find that they need to re-structure somewhere down the track. It makes good practical and business sense to separate your various assets into different structures, according to whether they are personal or business assets and further between depreciating and appreciating assets.

When you first set off on a new business venture, you don't want to assume that something will go wrong — but you do need to prepare and plan for the unforeseen. As well as that, you should in fact plan to be significantly successful. By setting up your ownership structure correctly, you minimise your exposure to risk so that if anything ever does go wrong, there is no impact on your personal assets or wealth. To change this down the track exposes you to potential additional expenses such as capital gains tax and stamp duty.

When operating your business, you should implement procedures and processes that limit your risks and exposure to litigation. You can achieve this by ensuring you act responsibly and within the laws, and also by taking out appropriate insurances, but your final safety net is to run your business through an appropriate ownership structure. This way, if any unforeseen events occur, your other assets are not exposed to litigation or loss.

Essentially, what you're doing is creating a 'safe harbour' for your wealth to ensure that the wealth stays within the family (intergenerational wealth) with an additional benefit of not exposing your wealth and assets to any sort of risk. As a side note, you should also be aware that the 'goodwill' and intellectual property and trademarks you create in your business are valuable assets and must also be protected.

Beyond risk and asset protection, there are many other important and practical reasons why you need to use the most appropriate ownership structure for your business. These include:

1. Estate planning
2. Wealth creation
3. The impact income tax might have on your cash flow
4. Capital Gains Tax (CGT), particularly if you sell or introduce new partners (including family members)

5. An efficient and effective mechanism to pass assets on to the next generation

6. Flexibility

## WHERE TO BEGIN

The main structures for owning and operating a business are loosely grouped into four categories:

1. Sole trader

2. Partnership

3. Company

4. Trust

There are advantages and disadvantages of all of the above, but the majority of business owners operate under options 3 or 4: a company or a trust. At Chan & Naylor we seldom recommend trading under options 1 and 2, as a sole trader or partnership, as these structures don't effectively manage or address estate planning, flexibility and asset protection concerns. In the case of partnerships, this also exposes both parties to the acts of the other party.

Sole trader is the simplest structure and is used by many business owners. Under this structure, all income (after deducting all business-related expenses) is taxed at the sole trader's personal marginal income tax rate. Capital gains on a sale of the business or its assets would go to the sole trader and the 50% CGT general discount rules would apply. Sole traders must apply for an Australian Business Number (ABN) and tax file number. Being a simple structure, both the operating costs and the administrative requirements will be minimised.

However, this structure provides no asset protection and, if anything goes wrong in the business, all personal assets are also exposed. All income and capital gains would be attributed to the sole trader and there is no flexibility on the distribution of income or capital gains.

A similar situation exists with partnerships. This type of structure puts every partner at risk for the actions of each of the other partners. Therefore, the actions of Partner A can impact Partner B and his assets. There are some benefits to this structure; if you are a husband and wife team, for example, it allows for the income to be distributed as you wish based on a fixed agreement.

However, in most cases, the benefits of running your business as a partnership are far outweighed by the potential risks. Note that you can have partnerships between individuals, companies and/or trusts, but the underlying issue for most is that each party will be liable for the actions of the other party you are in partnership with. There may be benefits including tax planning for a small business person to be in partnership with a spouse and specific advice is required.

Therefore, for the remainder of this chapter we will focus our attention on company and trust ownership structures.

## CONSIDERATIONS — GST & PSI

Before contemplating starting a business, the issues of Goods and Services Tax (GST) and Personal Services Income (PSI) need to be considered.

All businesses, irrespective of structure, must register for an ABN. Although it isn't mandatory, we recommend that business owners also register their business name with the respective state government agency.

## GOODS AND SERVICES TAX (GST)

In summary, GST is a 10% tax applied to the gross revenue invoiced, less any GST paid on the goods or services acquired to provide the sale that generated the gross sales revenue. You need to add 10% to your base selling price, which must be paid to the ATO (irrespective of whether you make a profit), less any GST you paid on your inputs.

If your business activities will generate more than $75,000 gross income per financial year, then the business must register for GST. When reviewing your GST position, you need to become familiar with the following terms:

- **Registration**: You must register for GST if you carry on an enterprise (business) and the revenue from your business activities exceeds $75,000 pa.

- **Taxable Supply**: GST is payable on each sale. The supplier must be registered and operating an enterprise, and the supply must be for consideration and primarily in Australia. It must not be GST Free or Input Taxed.

- **Input Tax Credits (ITC)**: The GST paid by your business and claimed back on taxable supply sales. **Input Taxed Supplies**: The sale of goods and services where GST does not apply and the supplier cannot claim credits for any GST paid on their own acquisitions. E.g. financial services and residential property.

- **GST Free**: No GST is payable on the purchase but the supplier is entitled to claim credits for the GST payable on its acquisition.

- **Tax Invoice**: To be able to claim ITC, your acquisition must be supported by a tax invoice showing the supplier's ABN and price breakdown, identifying the GST component.

- **Input Taxed Supplies**: The sale of goods and services where GST does not apply and the supplier cannot claim credits for any GST paid on their own acquisitions. E.G. financial services and residential property.

## PERSONAL SERVICES INCOME (PSI)

PSI refers to any income generated by personal exertion. In other words, it is income that is mainly a reward for an individual's personal efforts or skills, and it must be attributed to them personally for tax purposes.

You qualify as a personal services business if any of the following applies to your situation:

1. You meet the results test:

   a. Income is paid to achieve a specified result or outcome;
   b. You provide the necessary tools and equipment (if required) to do the work; and
   c. You are liable for rectifying defects in the work. If, in a given income year, 75% or more of your personal services income meets all three conditions, you pass the results test for that year.

OR

2. Less than 80% of your personal services income in the financial year comes from each client, and you meet one of the other three personal services business tests (the unrelated clients test, employment test or business premises test).

OR

3. You obtain a determination from the Australian Tax Office confirming that you are a personal services business.

### COMPANY OWNERSHIP STRUCTURE

The majority of businesses operate out of a company. A company is a separate legal identity in the eyes of the law. Therefore,

it separates the business operations from the individual, providing a layer of asset protection. In limited circumstances, the directors of a company can be held personally liable for the actions of the company, such as if a company operated while insolvent, or the directors engaged in fraudulent acts.

A Proprietary Limited (Pty Ltd) company is only required to have one director and one shareholder. It is governed by the rules of the company, called the 'Constitution'. The tax rate of a company is a flat rate, which is currently 27.5% for businesses with turnover under $50 million (current as of publication date; check www.ato.gov.au for the most up to date information).

All income and assets belong to the company and if you would like to withdraw funds from a company, you can do so by either paying a salary or via the payment of a dividend to the shareholders after you pay the appropriate tax.

If you own your business in a family company structure, this means that the company is owned by individuals. In this case, each individual holds an asset (shares in the company) and these assets would be available to creditors in the event of litigation. The loss of the shares could mean the loss of income and a valuable asset to the individuals.

Asset protection is not a normal benefit of a company structure, as a company only offers limited liability. This means that if the company is sued, only the assets within the company are available to creditors and normally shareholders are not required to fund any additional amounts. Directors, as previously explained, can be exposed under limited circumstances. If the shareholder is successfully sued they could lose their shares and therefore part of their wealth.

The following diagram sets out the most common basic ownership structure for a family company.

**XYZ Pty Ltd**

XYZ Pty Ltd Operates Business

**Shareholders or Members**

- Person A Dad – one ordinary share (being 50%)
- Person B Mum – one ordinary share (being 50%)

**Office Holders**

- Person A Dad, who works in the business – Director and Secretary
- Person B Director. This could be Mum, but we would not recommend this as she would be pulled into any litigation and as a result, family assets such as your family home would be more at risk. Instead, just have Dad (who operates the business) as the only director.

As a basic example, if $100 net profit was generated:

- The company receives $100
- Tax is paid at the company rate of 27.5%, which is $27.50
- The remaining $72.50 profit is distributed to shareholders, with $36.25 going to person A and $36.25 going to person

- B. The split of dividends depends on the number of shareholders and their individual percentage ownership of ordinary shares
- Because the $72.50 was paid after XYZ Pty Ltd paid
- Australian tax on all its earnings, the $72.50 dividend is said to be 'fully franked'

As you can see from the cash-flow perspective above, you are required to pay tax before you receive any money to do other things, such as invest.

The shareholders also receive the money in the form of a dividend, which can be 'franked' (meaning tax has been paid at the company rate of 27.5%) or 'unfranked' (meaning no tax has been paid).

Shareholders are then required to pay the appropriate amount of tax according to their income tax bracket. However, if they receive a franked dividend, they will also receive a credit for the tax that has already been paid by the company. This can become complicated, so if you use this ownership structure, it's worthwhile discussing these matters with your accountant before the end of financial year.

When choosing the best ownership structure for your business, it's worth taking into account your future plans in regards to selling the business.

CGT is a tax that is payable upon the sale of an income- producing asset, such as a business or a piece of real estate. Individuals are entitled to a 50% discount on the amount of CGT that is payable if they hold on to the asset for at least 12 months. A company, however, is not entitled to receive the 50% CGT discount.

If you sell your business the buyer will normally not want to buy the shares, as they will then take on any liabilities in the company. Therefore, the company sells the assets including goodwill and receives cash in return.

The capital profit is attributed to the company, which does not qualify for the 50% CGT discount. The problem that then arises is, how do you get access to the funds? Unfortunately you normally need to pay higher tax, as the extraction of the funds is a complex matter. Prior to any company sale, you should consult your tax accountant for advice.

There are many other complex issues associated with CGT and company structures, not limited to the fact that it is relatively difficult to get the profits out of the company and into your hands without paying additional tax. Therefore, if a client decides to use a company to operate their business, we recommend the following structure:

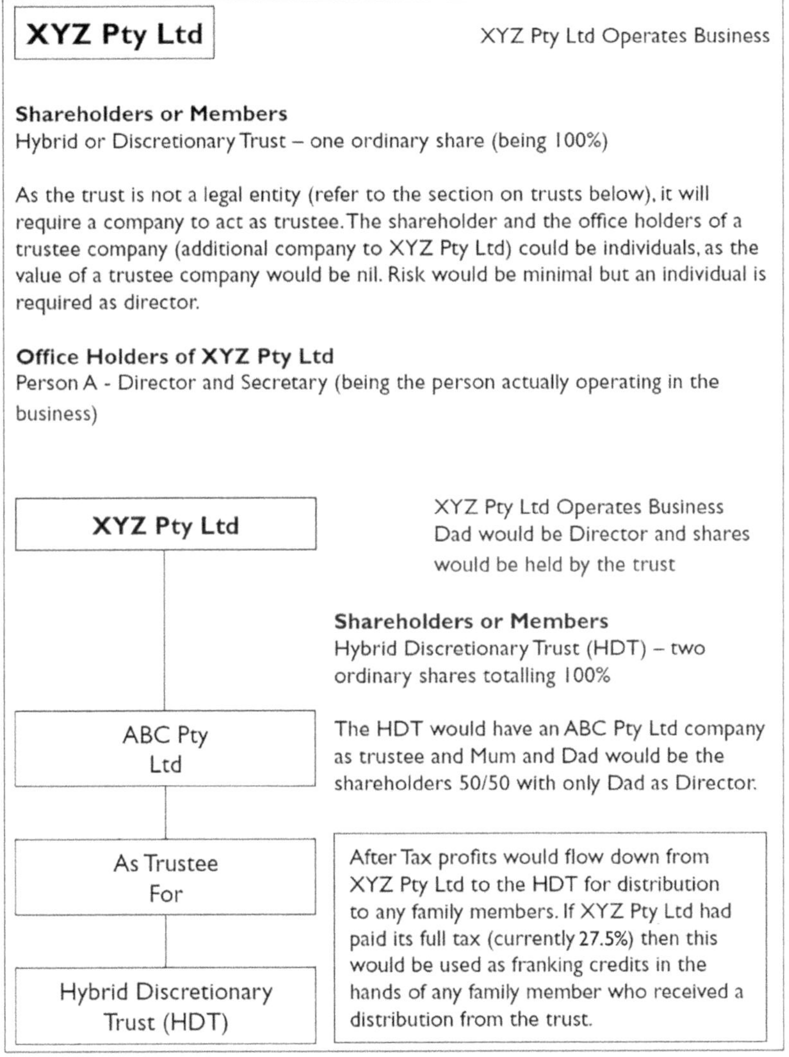


In this structure, we have replaced the shareholder with a trust for the following reasons:

1. More flexibility when distributing dividends to trust beneficiaries, which allows for better management of tax planning (keep in mind that it is still utilising after- tax funds).

2. Better asset protection, as the shares of the company are held in the trust. In the event that the individuals are sued, they are not holding an asset in their own names.

3. More flexibility in relation to capital gains treatment when the business is sold.

When the business is sold, the trust (being the shareholder) will receive the profits, which can then be distributed to any beneficiary. Note that similar limitations apply to the trust shareholder as for the individual, in relation to the company distributing either dividends or capital on liquidation. There are still the same issues in that the company does not receive the 50% CGT discount, but the main advantage is that the shares are not owned by individuals, but by a trust. If the shares on xyz are sold then the shareholder receives the 50% CGT discount but this rarely happens due to the risks to the new owner.

Given the complexity and inflexibility, not to mention the adverse tax consequences, of operating the business via a company structure, Chan & Naylor would not normally advise clients to use a company structure, even with a trust as shareholder. We believe that a trust offers the most benefits to business owners in almost every field.

## TRUST OWNERSHIP STRUCTURE

The main benefit of a trust structure is that it provides flexibility. Income can be distributed to the lower income earner, assets can be protected and wealth can be passed on to the next generation with minimal fuss and little or no tax payable.

To be clear, a trust is not a legal entity; it is basically an agreement or promise. It is also a vessel that holds assets on behalf of beneficiaries.

Put simply, a trust is simply an agreement (trust deed) between a trustee (the legal owner) and beneficiaries (beneficial owner) that in the event of certain things happening, certain things will occur.

For example, the agreement might be that if the trust generates profits from business activities, then the trustee can distribute this profit to beneficiaries at its discretion, and each beneficiary will then pay the appropriate amount of tax according to their personal situation.

It is critical to understand that the trust owns the assets — not the beneficiaries or decision makers. Therefore, if these beneficiaries find themselves in litigation, then the trust assets are not available to creditors.

Also, as it is the trust that is generating the income (subject to PSI rules), the trust cash flows can be distributed to beneficiaries in any proportion.

Trusts come in all shapes and sizes and there is no 'one size fits all' structure. The type of trust that is most suitable for you and your business depends on many factors, such as the type of asset or business, financing, income type, marriage status, and susceptibility to being sued.

Be wary of anyone that says, "such-and-such trust will suit all situations", because that is simply not true. Typical trust types include family, discretionary, unit, fixed, hybrid, Property Investors Trust (PIT) and Superannuation.

A trust is a legal document (the deed) that explains how assets are to be treated. Therefore, the rules identified within the trust deed formalise what sort of trust it is, not the label used to describe it. It is only as good as the rules that someone wrote.

A trust is essentially an agreement in which a person or company agrees to hold assets for the benefit of another. The one who holds the assets is called the trustee; those who benefit are called beneficiaries.

## POSITIONS IN A TRUST

There are four main positions in a trust structure:

1. **Trustee** — the decision maker

2. **Beneficiary or principal** — the receiver of the benefits

3. **Appointer** — the person who decides who the trustee will be. Without doubt, this is the real position of power

4. **Settlor** — the person who helps set up the trust. Note that once the trust is set up, the settlor plays no further role. Typically the settlor gives $10 to set up the trust. Not all trusts require a settlor, only those with discretion.

A typical trust used in business by a family group is as follows:

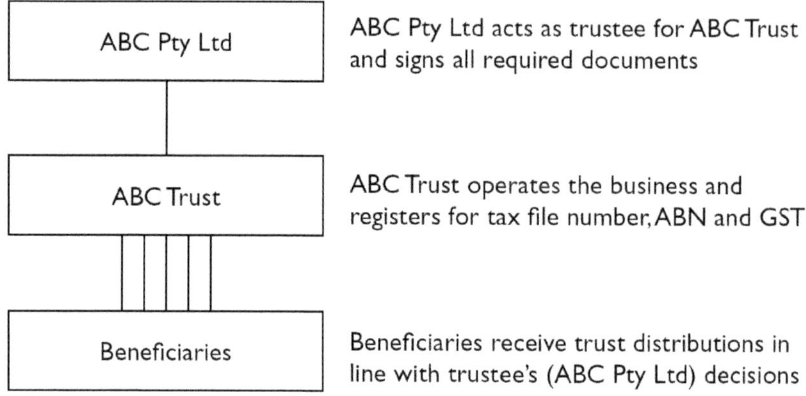


The trustee has legal control, which is legal title only. A person with legal control can buy and sell an asset but will never own or enjoy the benefits of ownership, such as income or usage. It's the trustee's name that appears on all legal documents, bank accounts, etc. As previously discussed, it would be recommended that only those family persons operating the business be directors.

The beneficiaries are not all necessarily mentioned in the trust deed. They have beneficial ownership (allowing a person to enjoy the benefits of ownership, including usage, income, profits, etc) and are entitled to the assets and profits of the trust. People normally specifically named are the principal people. The trust deed typically captures by category (such as children, parents etc) all relatives, companies and trusts associated with them and the spouses of those people.

## THE BASIC FUNCTION OF A TRUST

The basic function of a trust is to separate control and ownership. The result is that asset protection is possible and profits can be distributed in the most efficient way.

When you establish a trust of your own, you have both legal control and beneficial ownership. Most people don't separate the hats; they think they're one and the same, but they are not.

For example, asset protection occurs because even though legal title is in the name of Joe Bloggs, Joe is trustee for a trust and therefore doesn't actually own the assets. They are held in trust for the beneficial owners — hence nothing can be taken from Joe, because he doesn't legally own it.

Ownership plays a key factor in not just asset protection, but also estate planning and within the tax system too. This is why a star player will own nothing and control everything!

There are many benefits to operating your business via a trust structure that you can use to your advantage.

Given the special nature of running a business and allowing a follow-through to the next generation while creating maximum estate planning and asset protection, Chan & Naylor has developed a specific trust for business called a Business Enterprise Trust (BET). Our BET caters for the practical and commercial needs of running a business, and also allows you to grow and protect your assets from generation to generation. The BET covers the following:

1. It is capable of introducing new 'owners' including, but not limited to, family.

2. It allows for different beneficiaries.

3. It is possible to easily change appointers and trustees.

4. Any distributions can be restricted to family lineage, i.e. no in-laws.

5. It lasts over a long period of time. Trusts normally cease after 80 years; the BET has no end date.

6. It allows the business's appreciating assets — such as business real property, goodwill, intellectual property, etc — to be owned outside of the business and leased back to the B.E.T.

7. Easily allows for a distribution to another entity such as a trust where property as an example is held. The benefit of this is that if the trust with the property is negatively geared then pre tax money from the BET can be distributed (via family trust election) to the loss trust.

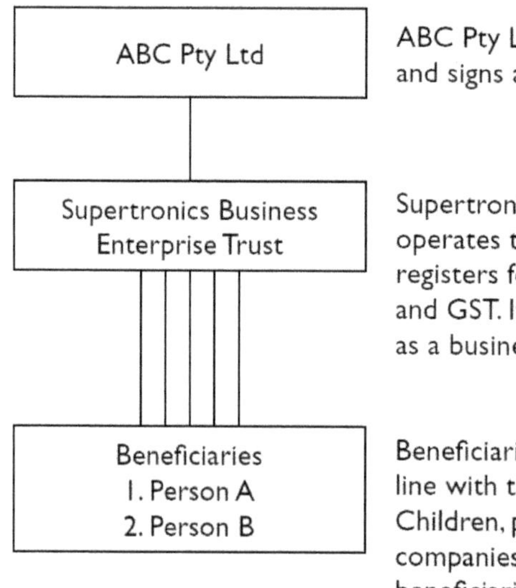


ABC Pty Ltd acts as trustee for ABC Trust and signs all required documents.

Supertronics Business Enterprise Trust operates the electronics retail business and registers for its own tax file number, ABN and GST. It may also register Supertronics as a business name.

Beneficiaries receive trust distributions in line with trustee's (ABC Pty Ltd) decisions. Children, parents, other relatives, associated companies and trusts are also captured as beneficiaries without specifically naming them. It would NOT be advisable to specifically name others.

If the profit (revenue less expenses) from this trust was $80,000, the distribution to beneficiaries could apply as follows (based on 2010/11 tax rates) given this is their only income:

1. Person A: $39,168 (tax $5,059.96)

2. Person B: $39,168 (tax $5,059.96)

3. Remainder to the four minor children: $416 each (tax nil)

The total tax payable on $80,000 is $8,700, or just under 11%. The tax calculations are correct as at the date of writing, but you should check the ATO website (www.ato.gov.au) for the tax rates that currently apply as they are subject to change.

Note that trust distributions to minors is heavily taxed to discourage income splitting, and low income tax offset will only reduce tax payable on excepted income. Trust distribution is not excepted income for minor therefore Low Income Tax Offset won't apply. The minor cannot achieve receiving $3,000 without tax. Income earned by minors through their personal exertions is taxed at adult tax rates.

Had the $80,000 been paid as dividends or partnership income to Person A and Person B, a total tax of just under $11,700 would have been payable, compared to approximately $8,700 via the trust.

Having said that, a trust should not be used solely to reduce tax, or Part IVA of the ATO's anti-avoidance rules would apply, and higher tax rates would be applicable. In this case, if Person A and B could demonstrate that a trust structure was used because they were concerned about asset protection, estate planning and a more efficient mechanism for wealth creation, then it is unlikely that the anti-avoidance legislation would apply.

As you can see from a cash-flow perspective, the profits of the business flow to the beneficiaries before any tax is paid, which is a significant and very important difference to the company structure — especially if you are an investor leveraging your assets via gearing. The primary advantages of using a trust structure, and in particular the BET, are clear, as it allows for:

1. Distributions of business profits before tax

2. The ability to plan and manage the timing of tax payments

3. Flexibility

4. Estate Planning

5. Asset protection

## PROTECTING BUSINESS ASSETS

Whatever structure you decide to use to operate your business through, you should consider separating the value or goodwill of the business from the trading entity itself. Many people, through no fault of their own, find themselves facing financial hardship, so if you are making a substantial investment in a business over many years, it makes sense to try and protect this in the event of unforeseen circumstances.

You should consider a separate structure to hold assets such as equipment, goodwill, intellectual property, databases, brands or anything of significant value. This separate entity simply enters into a commercial agreement and licenses the right to use the assets, or leases the ability to use the equipment, back to the business.

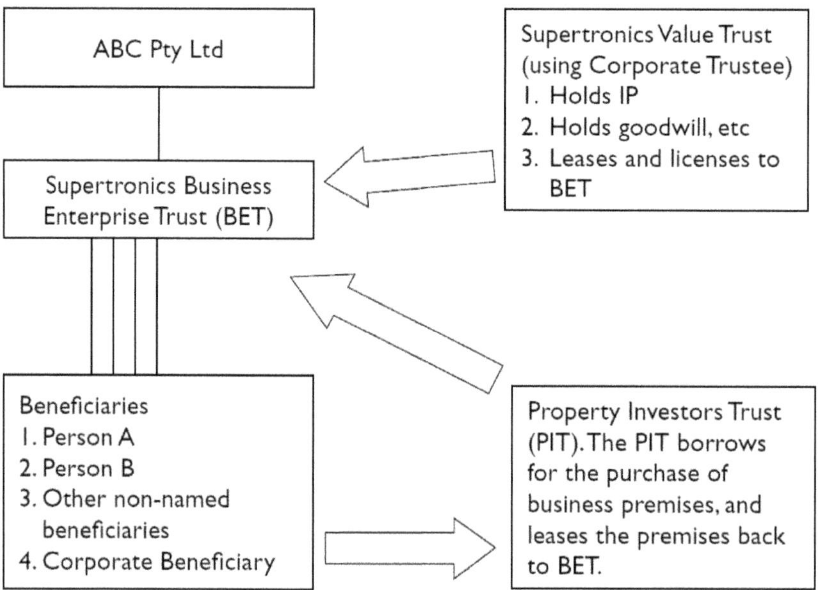


The above may seem a little confusing, but it works. This structure will allow the most flexible opportunity for growth and

dealing with unforeseen occurrences, while also benefitting you and your family by protecting the family assets and generating flexible distributions.

The starting point is the BET. The other structures can be added on as circumstances rollout. For instance, the Value Trust illustrated in this diagram will only be established if and when such assets are evident. For many businesses, the purchase of business premises and the creation of intellectual property may not eventuate from day one, but the BET allows for these 'bolt ons' to be added if and when required.

The ideal ownership structure for you will depend on your business and your situation, but you ideally want a structure that allows the business to grow uninhibited as your needs change. As always when it comes to complex legal and financial matters, you should always seek solid professional advice.

If you want to own and operate a business with third parties it may be appropriate to use a unit trust or derivative of the BET. Care is needed in drafting the unit trust as a court in some circumstances can look through to the beneficiaries to find any shortfall if the unit trust is successfully sued.

# PART 14
# Living the Dream

Hopefully, if you've made it this far, you now understand that it is possible to achieve your dreams by following the business philosophies in this book. If two very ordinary accountants and business owners can achieve this, then there's no reason why you can't too!

In these final chapters, we hope to inspire you to achieve great things and show you how you can transform your dream into reality. As mentioned at the beginning of this book, the Chan & Naylor business was launched in 1990 in a small office in Parramatta, with just three staff members: David Naylor, Ed Chan and a receptionist. The annual turnover was $50,000 and our business model looked like this:

***CHAN & NAYLOR — 1990***

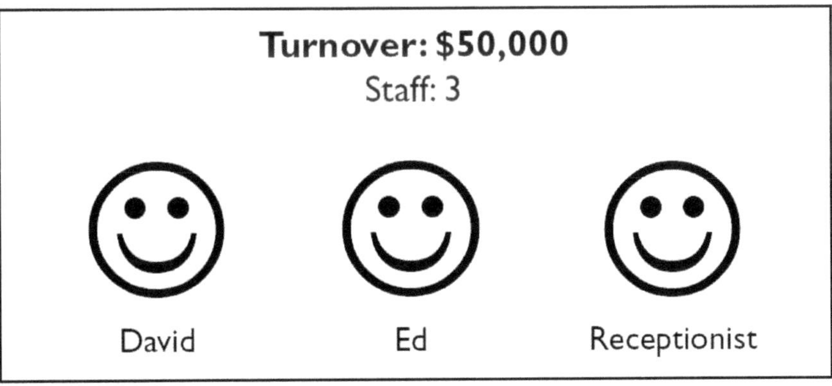


Today, two decades later, Chan & Naylor is a national group and a prominent brand in the professional services industry in Australia. We employ over 100 staff and achieve an annual turnover in excess of $14 million. Now, our model looks like this:

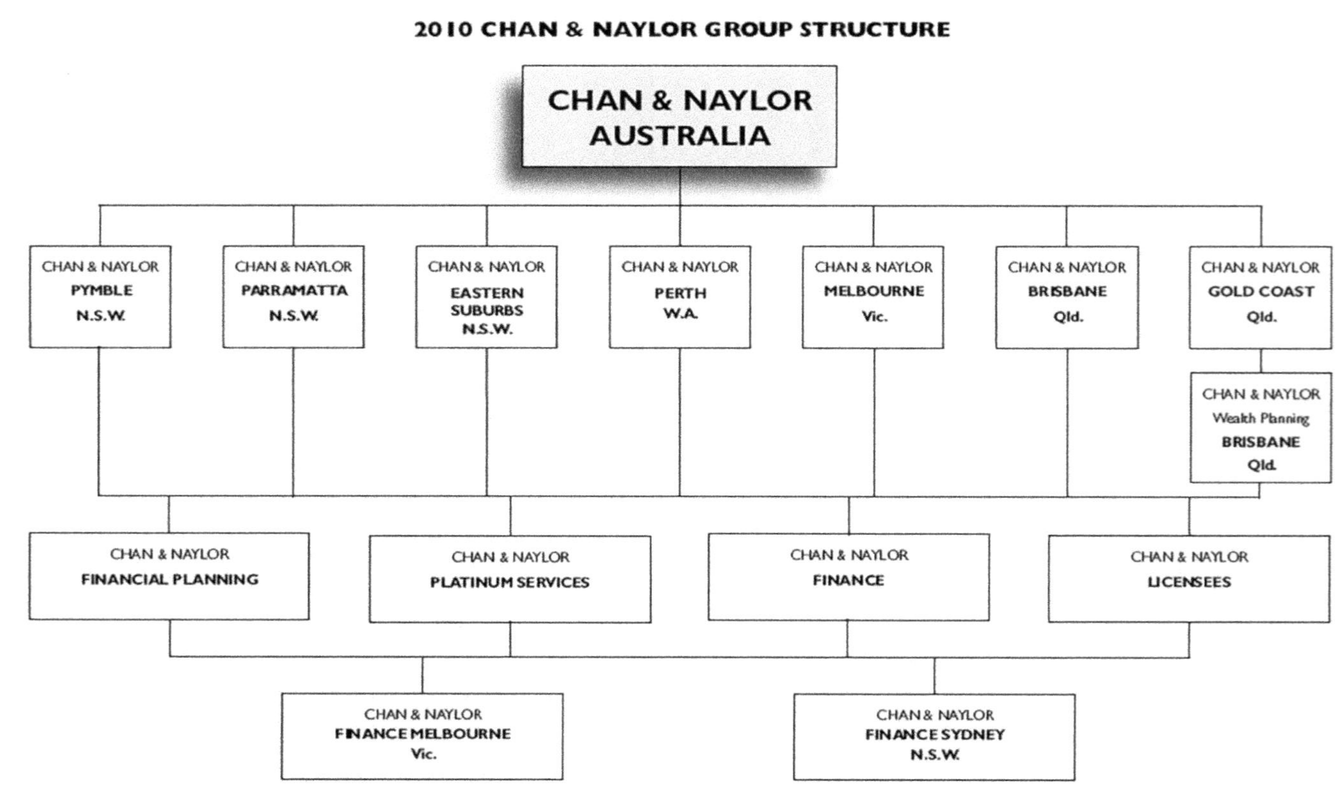
2010 CHAN & NAYLOR GROUP STRUCTURE
CHAN & NAYLOR AUSTRALIA
CHAN & NAYLOR PYMBLE N.S.W.
CHAN & NAYLOR PARRAMATTA N.S.W.
CHAN & NAYLOR EASTERN SUBURBS N.S.W.
CHAN & NAYLOR PERTH W.A.
CHAN & NAYLOR MELBOURNE Vic.
CHAN & NAYLOR BRISBANE Qld.
CHAN & NAYLOR GOLD COAST Qld.
CHAN & NAYLOR Wealth Planning BRISBANE Qld.
CHAN & NAYLOR FINANCIAL PLANNING
CHAN & NAYLOR PLATINUM SERVICES
CHAN & NAYLOR FINANCE
CHAN & NAYLOR LICENSEES
CHAN & NAYLOR FINANCE MELBOURNE Vic.
CHAN & NAYLOR FINANCE SYDNEY N.S.W.

## PURPOSE

What we have come to understand is that every being has a purpose – otherwise we would not exist.

Human beings have a specific purpose on this planet, which is to propagate otherwise we would die out. Individuals have other purposes. If you are a parent, for example, you have a purpose in life to raise your children and provide for them. Just like individuals have a purpose, so too do businesses and of course, businesses are made up of staff.

Each member of your team has a different purpose in life. As parents, partners, friends and colleagues, they have many diverse reasons to keep going. But, funnily enough, your team spends more of their waking time at work than they do with anything or anyone else.

So what is the purpose of your business and why do your team members turn up for work each day? Do they really, really understand their purpose and that of your business?

A large manufacturer of bricks underwent this exercise by asking its team, what is your purpose and why do you come to work every day?

The first answer was: to produce the bricks. We need to fire up the kiln and meet daily quotas on brick production.

The company questioned its team further...

**Question:** Well yes, that is what you physically do, but what does a brick do?
**Answer:** I suppose a brick builds a house.

**Question:** And what does a house do?
**Answer:** Provides shelter for someone.

**Question:** And by providing shelter for someone, what does that do?
**Answer:** Keeps people safe and warm, and provides for a good standard of living for individuals and families.

**Question:** Therefore, you are coming to work to...?
**Answer:** Produce a quality brick that will provide the foundations to build a house, which provides shelter and keeps people warm and safe, and improves the overall standard of living of our country.

It's a very motivating reason to come to work every day, wouldn't you agree?

At Chan & Naylor we went through a similar exercise with our team as we believe it's an important exercise so that both you as the owner and your team members understand the purpose of your business.

On the surface, yes, we are a firm of accountants specialising in property. However, we boast a unique point of difference. We prepare income tax returns, Profit and Loss statements and Balance Sheets for clients, but we also have strategies to help our clients build and create wealth.

Through these strategies and our ability to work with clients and their businesses proactively and holistically, we have an opportunity to help increase our clients' and our employees' net wealth. By increasing their average wealth, we will be able to contribute in some way to help raise standards of living in Australia. In theory if every country in the world was able to increase its net wealth, then we would be able to collectively raise the global standard of living.

China reduced its poverty levels from 300 million people in 2000 to 150 million in 2005, simply by increasing the average wealth of the population. As the country's overall wealth increased, the wealthier people in the country lifted the standard of living for the poor, which had the impact of reducing the poverty line — and, therefore, reduced the number of people living under the poverty level.

When we come to work each day, we are not simply preparing tax returns or financial accounts.

We are coming to work to:

"Build a national network of viable, expanding and exemplary models of Chan & Naylor offices across Australia to service and help our clients and our team increase their net wealth to the mutual benefit of all"

So what is the purpose of your business?

## THE BIGGER PICTURE

Now that you have read and understood our philosophies and the challenges we faced in growing our business, we would like to provide you with a 'bigger picture' look at what we believe are the fundamental principles of our success. These are the principles that override all else and, if you truly want to live your dream, these are not negotiable.

## LEADERSHIP — DO AS I DO

If you want to inspire people and earn their respect, you must lead by example, as you cannot expect someone else to do something that you are not prepared to do yourself.

There is an old saying that goes, "The fish stinks from the head down." Never has a truer word been spoken. We have found this to

be true across the board, whether it's referring to the headmaster of a school, the captain of a team or the CEO of an organisation.

At one stage, we were having great difficulty with the General manager of one of our branches. This person was running the business poorly and working very long hours, finishing most nights at 10pm, and coming in on Saturdays and Sundays as well.

However, despite the long hours, the business was still suffering. Turnover was dropping, clients were leaving, and although the manager was putting in the hours, it was clear that this person was more of a 'doer' than a 'manager'.

Once they left and a new General Manager was appointed, the whole business changed. It took 12 months to fully fix the problems, but the new General manager was a 'manager', not a 'doer', so they were able to effectively delegate and manage the staff, the clients and the workflow.

They worked regular 9–5 hours during the week and never came in on weekends, which just goes to show that you cannot grow a business by brute force. One can only grow a business via systems, training and effective delegation and management — and by having the right people in the right seats on the bus.

We've talked a lot about leverage throughout this book, and this example demonstrates that just as effective leverage of solid resources can bring you great rewards, leverage of mismanaged or ill-fitting resources — such as the wrong manager — can also bring you great harm.

This person's poor work practices soon became the work practices of the rest of the team, and the rest, as they say, is history.

When a business is performing poorly due to the practices of the manager, you will generally see significant changes happening within the first three months of leadership under a new manager. If this is not the case, then you might not have found the right fit with your new appointment.

We have also dealt with these kinds of issues at a more micro level. We had one particular client manager who managed around

$300,000 in fees, with two support staff members. That client manager struggled to manage their workload and, once again, would work enormous hours to try and hold the whole thing together. We tried to assist by providing training and support, but ultimately we had to remove the client manager.

We appointed a new client manager and within the first three months, they determined that the two support staff they had inherited did not have the ability to do the job competently. The Client manager asked that they be removed from their team and set about recruiting two new support staff.

Today, that client manager handles over $800,000 in fees and manages a team of four. Their effectiveness has lead to them handling a larger portfolio, while still only working 9–5 hours.

The ability to manage involves an ability to recruit the right people around you. In this situation, the original client manager didn't have the skill set to manage people, which meant that every time the support staff said they could not complete a task, the client manager would respond, "Leave it on my desk and I will finish it off for you."

The great leaders of our time and over history have always gained the respect of the people. Effective leadership is built on the art of helping people achieve common goals, and by recognising the contribution of others and encouraging them. You must always follow through with what you say and never over-promise and under-deliver — the eyes of the organisation are on your every move, so as the business owner you must take responsibility and set an example by going beyond the call of duty.

## EXPECT LONG-TERM REWARDS

We are sorry to be the providers of bad news, but those who tell you that a small business will give you a balanced and flexible lifestyle in the infancy and adolescence stages of growth are living in Disneyland — just ask any successful entrepreneur or successful business owner!

Initially, both of us put in enormous hours working over 100 hours a week, seven days a week, in order to build our business. Back then, holidays and sick days were unheard of.

These kinds of sacrifices have to be made if you want to be successful, as you only get out what you put in. While working long hours was not sustainable in the long term, we understood the concept that there is no such thing as a free lunch and there is no easy path to success — it comes down to plain old hard work. It's important to remember that the lifestyle will come later, when you are receiving a dividend from the many years of endeavour and sacrifice you have invested in your business.

## PLAN BACKWARDS

It's vital that you start with the end in mind. What is it you are building? Are you building a business that will give you a passive income stream? Are you building a business that you can later sell for a substantial capital gain? Do you want to create a business that will work so that you don't have to?

Be very clear about what type of business you are building and what you want your business to look and feel like. Whatever it is, you need a plan and it helps if you start with the end in mind and work backwards to where you are today. This will give you direction and a purpose.

Some people may need to call in the experts to help out with this planning. We did, and look where we are now! By turning to the experts and working through a Strategic Planning Session, we developed clear goals and plans for our business. It not only gave us direction, but it also helped to pull the whole team together, so that everyone was on the bus, in the right seat, looking to the future.

Unfortunately, many small companies have no vision for their business. They become rudderless and their employees have nothing to aim for. It's no wonder, then, that it all feels like a lot of hard work and everyone is 'dragging the chain'. Poor leadership creates a poorly performing business, as the 'fish surely stinks from the head down'.

## DELEGATE, DON'T ABDICATE

To be successful as a leader, business owner, manager or even a parent, you must follow this rule. The term 'abdicate' means to relinquish responsibility or power, whereas the term 'delegate' means to assign a duty, power or obligation to another. You must be clear on the difference between the two.

As leaders, we never relinquish our responsibility. However, as an organisation, we hire staff and assign duties, provide training, and implement systems and procedures to develop a culture.

When a mistake occurs at Chan & Naylor — and they do, because mistakes happen — we ask, "How can we fix the system so that it doesn't happen again?"

We don't blame the staff member, we blame the system, and to ensure that the problem doesn't happen again, we fix it by re- investing in training. Ultimately, the buck stops with us, and as leaders we never abdicate responsibility. However, we do delegate, delegate, delegate... this is the power of leverage.

The importance of delegation cannot be understated and yet when people abdicate, it can have the opposite effect. It happens all the time. For instance, have you ever heard one of your employees or colleagues say, "No, that's not my fault, I asked Jim to process that order," or, "That was Chris's job, I told him to pack away the stock before he left."

When you're a manager, you are responsible. Delegation involves taking responsibility for a task. You may delegate it to someone else to carry out, but the responsibility for the results rests with the person who delegated the job. They are ultimately accountable for the outcome.

Whenever we have witnessed poor performance within our business, it has usually boiled down to a person's inability to take responsibility. Instead, they abdicate their responsibility and the blame is laid at the feet of other people. Before long, a culture develops where everyone is blaming everyone else for any problems that arise.

These situations are often created when leaders have no clear vision of where the company is travelling, and therefore no clear responsibilities have been allocated to key people. This is why it's so crucial to make each person accountable for his or her Key Performance Indicators (KPI).

## LOOK, DON'T JUST LISTEN

This simple rule has had a significant impact on the growth and management of our business.

Whether it is sitting on the board of directors or dealing with your team, your client, your suppliers or even your family and children, it's vital that you don't just listen, but you actually investigate the situation.

Occasionally a staff member knocks on our door and makes a statement, comment or suggestion, and after further investigation we find that the statement was not actually factual. This could be due to a vested interest, a human emotion or a lack of understanding on someone's behalf.

As a manager, if you simply react to what is told to you at face value, you may end up making the wrong decision or taking the wrong course of action.

The same principle applies when you receive a complaint from a client or customer. It is easy to react when you have a client screaming abuse down the phone because of bad service and all you want to do is scream at a team member in response.

In actual fact, when you look into the situation and you speak with the team member involved, there may be a reasonable explanation, which then requires a simple explanation to the client. How many times have you been told one thing and then discovered it is completely opposite to the facts?

People often tell you what you want to hear, so when you listen, always make sure you look into the situation and check that what is being told to you is accurate, so you can make the best decisions for you and your business.

## BUILD CULTURE

We have discussed in detail the importance of culture in any organisation, and we hope that by now you can see how vital it is to your success. The way your people talk and look, the way they do things and the way the product or service is delivered is critical to the long-term survival of your business.

This responsibility ultimately rests with the leaders or owners, in the same way that as a parent, you are the leader of your family. In any family there are basic fundamental principles that you live by, such as having good manners and morals.

The same theory applies to your business. You as the leader must set out and enforce the culture and principles that your business operates under. Remember, if you do not follow and enforce the rules, you cannot expect anyone else to. Eventually it becomes second nature and is part of the fundamental core of the business.

In the early days of building the culture at Chan & Naylor, we introduced a uniform policy. It took some time for the team to fully embrace this concept, but once it was accepted, it became second nature to existing team members, and it is part of the recruitment process for new team members.

At the time we were one of the only accounting firms that had uniforms and when we attended external seminars as a group, it was very clear who we were. We had other people from other accounting firms approaching us to work with us, because they could see we had a strong culture.

Naturally, culture is not simply about having a uniform, but the uniform is a symbol of what we stand for. Culture is about the way we do things; it represents what we stand for and what clients can expect from us, and it gives those who deal with us some confidence about the manner in which we will act when they do business with us.

It also becomes our 'brand', which makes up the value proposition of what we offer. It's something that can be trusted and relied upon. Clients and customers are creatures of habit and they are far more likely to do business with you if you have a trusted and consistent brand and culture.

Inconsistency is the key cause of failure of most businesses. If you want proof of this, look at the success of franchises versus the success of small businesses: 80% of small businesses fail in the first five years, and yet the opposite is true for franchises, of which 80% succeed beyond the first five years.

## INVEST IN YOUR BALANCE SHEET

If you want to build and grow your business you must invest in the Balance Sheet. This may require a change in mindset, but the sooner you see that hiring a new staff member is an investment in your Balance Sheet — rather than a cost to your business — you'll begin to see that these decisions will pay dividends down the track. Over the years, as our business went through various cycles, we often had to re-invest to hire staff and introduce systems —

even to the point of reducing our personal income and going into overdraft. As a business owner, you must be prepared to take one step backwards in order to take two steps forward.

Most business owners are focussed on keeping costs to a minimum and, as a result, they are reluctant to spend money on things like staff training, database management and system building. However, this is short-term thinking — it's like trying to save money by not putting any oil in your car. Yes, the car will continue to drive in the short term, but eventually the engine will blow up and create huge problems and costs.

Every business can be run like ours — if there is a will, there is a way. The advantages are obvious:

1. Your income is no longer limited to the number of hours in the day. A successful business can generate generous profits for the owners, without the owners even having to turn up.

2. The business works without you, so you can take annual leave and sick leave while still earning income.

3. The business is worth a lot more money, because it does not depend on the owner to be successful.

4. You are able to improve your business because you can spend time working on the business, rather than doing the work to earn an income.

## IMPLEMENT, IMPLEMENT, IMPLEMENT

We have all heard the saying that success is comprised of 20% inspiration and 80% perspiration. This is a critical point when running a business, as we can all attend a meeting, go to seminars and read books, but none of this matters if you don't action what you learn.

A good idea or strategy is exactly that — a good idea or strategy. It only becomes worthwhile or valuable if the idea is put into action. Unfortunately, this is why many businesses fail, because the owners fail to roll up their sleeves and implement the plans and turn the ideas into action, whether through lack of skill or expertise, lack of resources, lack of focus or sheer laziness.

We have seen many organisation boards over the years and some do well and others fail. You will see that in our organisation board we have a division called "implementation". It's this division's responsibility to implement the ideas that the managing director comes up with. Again, the "implementation division" is an investment back into your business. Too many companies fail to invest back into their businesses, and then they wonder why the great ideas they had did not gather traction and momentum.

The success of your business depends on your ability to implement successfully, so if you do not have the skills or experience to implement something important, then make sure you source the appropriate outside help to get the job done.

## GIVE AND YOU WILL RECEIVE

In order for you to really launch your business growth and create a business that will have a life of its own, you must be prepared to give some of it away.

Most successful large corporations offer their employees an interest or equity in the company via an employee share scheme. In small business, we have found that in order to attract the right type of employee — those who are willing to work the hours, take ownership and drive the business that you created — you must be able to offer them some skin in the game. This could be in the form of equity or profit share bonuses.

We have always been of the belief that there needs to be a fair exchange for this to happen, and what we mean by "having skin in the game" is that the person risks his or her own money (which is that person's Balance Sheet investment) with the intention that through his or her drive, hard work and commitment, he or she will reap the benefits long term.

Many small business owners plan to sell their ownership in their business as a succession plan so they can invest their money elsewhere, while others prefer to leave their money in so they can receive a passive income stream (dividend) from their investment.

From our experience, we believe that skin in the game shows intent and is essential — and it's a model that works well. So for the right Abundant person, we are willing to share in the wins, as long as they are prepared to invest and have skin in the game.

## BE PERSISTENT & CONSISTENT

The term 'persistent' means refusing to give up or let go, and persevering insistently. The term 'consistent' means being unchanging in behaviour or beliefs, and always holding on to the same principles or practice.

You should apply these two basic principles to whatever you do in life, whether you're an athlete in training or playing sport, trying to lose weight, studying for exams, bringing up children or running a business.

The use of systems and uniforms are just a couple of means of delivering a consistent outcome, look and feel. They feed into the brand and culture in a consistent manner, and inspire confidence in your clients. When everyone is delivering the same service in 80% the same way, then you will get a loyal following.

Astheleaderandownerofyourbusiness, it is yourresponsibility to be persistent and consistent. However, you should also always be willing to listen and implement change in your organisation when necessary.

## UNDERSTAND THE POWER OF LEVERAGE

If you get nothing more out of this book than understanding the power of leverage, then you are already one step ahead of the game.

Leverage allows you to accelerate everything you do and transforms the equation so that 1 + 1 = 3.

If you have 11 ordinary athletes or football players in a team, and each member takes advantage of each other's strengths and weaknesses, you have a winning team. As a business owner, you leverage through your staff, your management, your strategic alliance partners and your co-owners or directors to create success.

We have already seen the value of having the right systems in place, for example the right recruitment system that sees that the right types of people get recruited. If you recruit the right type of people then you will be successful. If 80% of your business is systematised, the last 20% can be managed.

## DON'T LET EGO INTERFERE: "MY WAY OR THE HIGHWAY"

You have to know when to fight your battles and when not to, and unfortunately ego can stand in the way when you're trying to navigate this minefield.

In many ways, ego is an important ingredient in a successful entrepreneur and small business owner, but when you're making decisions, you have to put it aside for the betterment of your organisation.

You need to listen to staff and advisors and you may think that decisions made by others are wrong, or you may disagree with other opinions, and you are certainly entitled to express your thoughts. But when all is said and done and a decision needs to be made, don't allow your ego to interfere with the right decision. Sometimes, you have to swallow your pride in order to allow progress.

We have witnessed many profitable and successful businesses fall apart over the years due to the ego of the partner or business owner. They have cost themselves millions of dollars in future profits and gains, all for ego.

In one particular case, we had a business client that was making extraordinary profits, providing the owners with above-average wages and dividends and the business was growing at rapid rate.

They had other competitors in the industry who were jealous of their results. The only problem they had was, one partner wanted to take the business down a certain path, and the other partner disagreed and thought it should go in a different direction. They both dug their heels in and stood their ground and took the attitude that "it's my way or the highway".

Due to this difference in opinion and loss of focus, over a couple of years and after blowing hundreds of thousands of dollars in legal fees, the company ended up in the hands of an administrator. This multi-million dollar asset, which was providing a fantastic lifestyle to both of the owners, was now next to worthless — all due to the ego and stubbornness of the owners.

The worst thing about all of this was that if they had just come to an agreement in either direction, the business would have been very successful, regardless of which path they chose to travel down. As a business owner and a leader, it's important that you always focus on the bigger picture and ask yourself: "Is this decision going to get the organisation to where it should be in the next three, five or 10 years?"

If the answer is potentially yes, then you need to put your ego to the side, agree that it's the right move, and let the fruits of this decision feed your ego down the track.

# PART 15

# Listen to the Little Bird on Your Shoulder 'Life Balance'

Finding a balance in your life is difficult when running and building a small business , we can certainly attest to that, you are so busy caught up in the day to day stresses and pressures of running a Business you become programmed into living life a certain way and you neglect the other important areas of your life, family, friends, exercise, faith, whatever it is that is important to you.

Over the last 25 years we have had many learning experiences and hopefully we have become a little wiser ,we have also learnt by reading books (refer recommended reading) and we continue to learn each day, one such book had a significant impact.

"Tuesdays with Morrie" written by Mitch Albom is a story about An Old Man, a Young Man, and Life's Greatest Lesson".. In the book Morrie tells a little story that had an impact on both our lives and helped us refocus and bring back balance into our lives.

> *'Every day have an imaginary little bird on your shoulder that asks "Is today the day? Am I ready? Am I doing all I need to do? Am I being the person I want to be? ... when you are prepared to die, you are ready to live". Most of us walk around as if we are sleepwalking . we really don't experience the world fully because we are half asleep, doing things we automatically think we have to do. Everyone knows they're going to die, but nobody believes it. If we did, we would do things differently and be more involved in life while you're living.* "**Tuesdays with morrie**"

During your busy day take some time to listen to that imaginary little bird so you can also enjoy the important things in your life.

## CONCLUSION

Where you are today is a consequence of the decisions you made in the past, and where you end up in the future will be a consequence of the decisions you make today.

As Chan & Naylor moves into a new phase of expansion and business growth over the coming years, we will surely come across new challenges and issues and we will be confronted with difficult decisions.

The success of your business, and ours, will be a direct result of the actions that we take. We hope that in some way, the strategies and advice outlined in this book will help to guide and inspire you towards creating a business that delivers profits and creates wealth, and allows you to make the right decisions and live the dream you've created for yourself.

It's a road worth travelling, but it is certainly **a balancing act.**

We leave you with a verse that has inspired us over the years and is a constant reminder of the challenges we face each day.

We hope your business becomes a winner and we wish you all the best.

Good Luck!

**Ed Chan and David Naylor Chan & Naylor**

**A Winner's Creed**

If you think you are beaten, you are,

If you think you dare not, you don't

If you'd like to win,

But think you can't

It's almost certain you won't

If you think you'll lose, you're lost,

Since out in our world we find

Success begins with a person's will,

It's all in the state of mind.

Life's battles don't always go

To the stronger or faster hand,

They go to the one who trusts

And always thinks "I can"

## WE WOULD APPRECIATE YOUR FEEDBACK

Our aim is to help small business owners help themselves we would love to hear from you and your thoughts on the book and even the success you have achieved with your own business.

Our inspiration is your success.

Please email Ed and David on info@chan-naylor.com.au with any feedback, thoughts or comments or visit

- **www.chan-naylor.com.au**

**Chan & Naylor** is a National Property Accounting Group ranked in BRW's Top 100 Accountancy Firms in Australia. Established over twenty years ago by Edward Chan & David Naylor, Chan & Naylor was also named BRW's fastest- growing accountancy practice for two years running — in 2007 & 2008.There are Chan & Naylor offices in most major cities — including Melbourne, Sydney, Perth, Gold Coast and Brisbane.

The secret of their success is, unlike 99% of Accounting Firms, Chan & Naylor specialise in Property. With this focus Chan & Naylor are committed to service, knowledge and meeting their client's needs. They are recognised for their cutting edge property, business and tax solutions to meet their client's challenges.

Training of staff with systems and procedures has helped facilitate the rapid growth Chan & Naylor have experienced.The use of business coaches has proved instrumental in ensuring that not only all the partners are aligned but also the quality and culture is maintained throughout all the offices. Chan & Naylor as a group has a strong culture. Their staff are productive and enthusiastic.

At Chan & Naylor, you can count on their knowledge in the following areas: tax strategies; small business; structuring for property investment; self managed superfund structures; accounting services; and leading edge strategies around asset protection and wealth creation — particularly via property investing, estate planning and tax planning.

Chan & Naylor have become the **country's** premier specialist accountants in the area of property, and within the firm they have nurtured an expertise that rival — and even surpasses — some of the largest Accountancy firms in Australia.

Even partners of the largest accountancy and law firms come to us for their own personal accountancy needs in this area. Chan and Naylor **prepare tax returns for over 10,000 clients.**

Chan & Naylor is the model firm studied by thousands of students when undertaking their CPA studies from the Australian Society of Certified Practicing Accountants and students completing their MBA at Queensland University.

If you would like to contact the business coaches used by **Chan & Naylor** please email info@chan-naylor.com.au

The Chan & Naylor motto is

*"To help our clients increase and protect their net worth from generation to generation"*

**Contact Chan & Naylor now!**

**1300 250 122**

**Ask the Experts**

A free 10 min Question and Answer service is provided by Chan & Naylor to new clients.To register your business, property, finance or tax question please visit

**https://www.chan-naylor.com.au/contact-us/**

*Call Chan & Naylor to make an appointment to discuss your business, property tax  and accounting. For office locations please visit www.chan-naylor.com.au*

www.ingramcontent.com/pod-product-compliance
Ingram Content Group UK Ltd.
Pitfield, Milton Keynes, MK11 3LW, UK
UKHW020118200726
13856UKWH00002B/605